THE
CIVILIZATION
OF THE
RENAISSANCE

LEONARDO DA VINCI: ADORATION OF THE MAGI

THE CIVILIZATION OF THE RENAISSANCE

By
JAMES WESTFALL THOMPSON
GEORGE ROWLEY
FERDINAND SCHEVILL
GEORGE SARTON

FREDERICK UNGAR PUBLISHING CO.
NEW YORK

First published 1929

Republished 1959

Printed in the United States of America

Library of Congress Catalog Card No. 58-59873

TABLE OF CONTENTS

LIST OF ILLUSTRATIONS

FOREWORD

The real meaning and significance of a great civilization is not to be discovered in any one expression of its life. Neither its art nor its business nor its science nor even its literature alone can reveal the heart of its life. To find this the student must study all of its parts so that he may see it whole.

When the Alumnae Association of Mount Holyoke College made possible the Mary Tuttle Bourdon Lectures, the College decided that the first year should be devoted to the Renaissance, and invited a group of scholars, each distinguished for his contributions to some one aspect of the field, to present successively the civilization we have learned to call a new birth.

The enthusiasm with which the project was undertaken by the several participants made a vivid picture which proved stimulating in its contrasts. The lectures are reproduced here substantially as they were given.

EXPLORATION AND DISCOVERY
DURING THE RENAISSANCE

EXPLORATION AND DISCOVERY
DURING THE RENAISSANCE

JAMES WESTFALL THOMPSON

IN THE immortal prologue to Herodotus' immortal *History* these words may be read: "These are the researches of Herodotus of Halicarnassus which he publishes in the hope of thereby preserving from decay the remembrance of what men have done, and of preventing the great and wonderful deeds of the Greeks and Barbarians from losing their due meed of praise."

It is in this spirit that I come before you this evening, with the wish to relate the tale of discovery and exploration in the pulsing period of the Renaissance as briefly and clearly as I may. And may I express the hope, borrowing a sentence from the noble Prologue of Froissart's *Chronicle*, that "I may continue and persevere in such wise that whoso this process readeth or heareth, may take paustance, pleasure and ensample" therefrom.

In a very famous sentence the French historian Michelet described the Renaissance as "the discovery of the world and of man." By it he meant to say that the mind of the Renaissance had ceased to be supremely interested in heaven and hell, as men were in the Age of Faith, but instead that men were ardently interested in the immediate world around them; that thought had become secularized; that theology and the scholastic philosophy, in so far as they continued to hold the boards, did so in virtue of authority and tradition, but that the normal man was more absorbed with his own individual experience and with experiential methods than with "otherworldliness."

It is possible, however, to use Michelet's phrase in another sense, namely, as one descriptive of geographical discovery and exploration of new lands and new peoples. This is the sense in which I shall employ it. For one of the most important and striking manifestations of the Renaissance was its passionate interest in remote and hitherto unknown lands and peoples, and the courageous and adventurous spirit which emboldened Europe to penetrate into them. Central and Far Asia, Mongolia, Cathay, India, the Malay Peninsula and Archipelago, Central and seaboard Africa became part of the immediate and concrete knowledge of cultured Europe. Even Australia was not unknown, and its modern discovery actually was but rediscovery. Between 1250 and 1500 the physical horizon of mankind was widened far beyond the achievements of any previous or subsequent period of discovery. It is certainly no exaggeration to say that the progress of geographical discovery and exploration, with the simultaneous broadening of the intellectual horizon, forms one of the most important manifestations of the Renaissance.

Like every other great historical movement this movement, too, had varied and remote sources of origination. Politics and religion, commerce and trade, zeal for the acquisition of new scientific knowledge, the sheer spirit of adventure, which Tennyson has so admirably described in *Ulysses*, all entered into and promoted the movement. Before the eyes of these bold spirits gleamed "an untravelled world whose margin fades forever and forever." To find Cathay was the hope of all their dreams. Some sought it by going eastward across Asia. Others sought to find it by the sea-route westward—"to sail beyond the sunset and the baths of all the western stars."

The inception of the movement of discovery and exploration must be found in the Crusades, the earliest great expansion of Christian Europe, which for the first time brought the West into intimate contact with new lands and new peoples. The Crusades introduced the period of discovery and exploration which ultimately led to the finding of a new world. More intimate knowledge of the Near

East created a craving for more knowledge of the Far East, whether Cathay or India.

The initiative in the thirteenth century, however, did not emanate from merchants or conquerors, nor even from adventurers, but from the Franciscan friars. It may seem grotesque to say, yet I say it seriously, that St. Francis of Assisi did more to initiate the age of discovery and exploration than any other single person. By 1200 the futility of the Crusades was abundantly manifest. The Holy Land had been lost in 1187. The kingdom of Jerusalem was a thing of shreds and patches. It was evident that Christendom could not hold its own in a military capacity against Islam. Untold blood and treasure had been spent in vain. Moreover, the Crusades had given birth to appalling bloodshed and intolerance, and the bad blood between West and East was black with hatred. The condition shocked St. Francis, who loved all mankind, even heathen and infidels, and to whom war was the basest of human activities. For St. Francis is the greatest of all pacifists.

In the heart of St. Francis was born the hope to make the Crusades unnecessary by peaceful and loving effort to convert the Mohammedans to Christianity. Thereby St. Francis also became the patron saint of all missionaries. Accordingly in 1219, having divided the world among his disciples and reserved Syria and the Holy Land for himself, St. Francis embarked for Egypt. From this base the Grey Friars began their missionary labors in the Mohammedan world. The Franciscans were the first Europeans who acquired immediate and accurate information of the lands and peoples beyond the pale of Christendom. Their labors were more successful in this capacity than in making converts.

But in the middle of this century an event befell which called the Franciscan missionaries from the Near East into Central and Farther Asia. This was the Mongol conquest of all Asia except India, and of Eastern Europe as well, and their union into a formidable empire. The disaster of Wahlstat in 1241 showed that Europe was militarily incapable of coping with the Mongol conquerors, and that Central and Western Europe had been spared owing to the Mongols' moderation in not extending their advance beyond Russia. In this crisis Pope Innocent IV and St. Louis of France separately conceived the idea of sparing Europe from Mongol conquest, and at the same time checkmating Mohammedanism by attempting to convert the Mongols to Christianity. It was grandiose strategy.

This hope was not as fantastic as it may seem. For by the side of their racial shamanism, almost every Asiatic religion was represented in the Mongol army—Mohammedans, Buddhists, and what not. Hulagu, the grandson of Ghenghiz Khan, was a Buddhist, but his wife was a Nestorian Christian. The presence of many Christians among the Mongols was known. In a word, the Mongols were tolerant of all religions provided they did not play politics.

Accordingly in 1245 an embassy from the pope left Europe for Farther Asia to visit the Great Khan, whose seat was at Karakorum, four hundred miles south of modern Irkutsk, and the Mongol imperial capital until the conquest of China by Kubla Khan. The head of this papal embassy was John of Plan-Carpini, a friar minor and friend of St. Francis. Having first visited the Mongol chieftain of the Golden Horde on the Volga in order to get passports and interpreters, Plan-Carpini set out on April 8, 1246, to cross Asia, following the Great Overland Road, the oldest overland road in history, along which from time immemorial have passed the silk and the jade of China to the Occident. But do not picture to yourselves a Lincoln Highway. This oldest and longest road in history started from Peking, crossed the Gobi desert to Karakorum, and passed on over the tremendous "divide" between the Altai and the Tian-Shan Mountains by a pass 15,000 feet high. A modern traveler who has followed its course has described those

astonishing gorges . . . . of a strange and sinister splendor, of a withering heat and a burnt dark ugliness. Deep between black walls and buttresses of precipices the perilous track goes climbing along the sheer faces; far over head rise close on either side lifeless crags on which occasional mica smears give a delusive look of moisture to their arid altitudes; where the only sign of life is the asphodel, itself like the ghost of a corpse-candle aspiring in millions of diaphanous pale flames from all the sombre walls of the gorge.

In Turkestan the road divided, one branch continuing to Persia and the Mediterranean ports, the other to Russia, where Kiev and Novgorod were its termini.

So much for scenery. What of distances? Asia is the greatest of the continents, roughly measuring 110 degrees of longitude. This at 60 miles to a degree would make the distance from Korea to the tip of Asia Minor more than 6,500 miles, or twice the width of the United States. If the Mongol Empire were superimposed upon the United States it would extend from Maine to Hawaii.

All the way from Kiev to Karakorum, across wind-swept plateaus, over stupendous mountain ranges, through fervent heat and wintry blizzards, among strange and sometimes savage peoples, these four intrepid sons of St. Francis plodded their way with sandaled feet, walking every step of the way in single file, as Dante has described them, "one in front and one behind," for like their master they refused to ride even so much as a mule. At last Plan-Carpini reached the barbarously magnificent court of Guyuk, Ghenghiz Khan's grandson and Great Khan himself. Time fails me to tell of all he saw and learned. But Plan-Carpini returned to write in his official *Relation* the earliest European account of the land and the peoples of Central and Farther Asia, anticipating Marco Polo's travels by more than a half-century.

Carpini had not completed the writing of his *Relation* when in 1252 St. Louis at St. Jean d'Acre in the Holy Land, independently of what Pope Innocent IV had undertaken, resolved to send an ambassador of his own choice to the Grand Khan and upon precisely the same mission. This was another Franciscan, but a Belgian, not an Italian, named William of Ruysbroeck. He, too, reached Karakorum. His *Relation* divides honors with that of Carpini. He proved that the Caspian Sea was a lake without outlet, whereas the belief in Europe was that it had connection with the Arctic Ocean by some mysterious river. But perhaps the most interesting information afforded by Ruysbroeck is that about the many Europeans whom he found dwelling in the heart of Asia under Mongol rule. At Karakorum he found a young French matron named Paquette, from Metz, who had married a Russian and with him had been taken prisoner when the Mongols captured Kiev. Her husband was then an architect in the service of Guyuk. Another such was a former Parisian goldsmith named Guillaume Le Boucher, whose brother then had a shop upon the Grand Pont. Master William had been captured at Belgrade, had married a Hungarian woman, and was the chief goldsmith of the Great Khan. Ruysbroeck even encountered an Englishman out there, but one who had been born in Hungary. So far as we know these two Franciscan friars were the first Europeans to bring back direct ocular information of Farther Asia. Like the Jesuits in North and South America in the seventeenth and eighteenth centuries they were at once missionaries and explorers. The travels of Carpini and Ruysbroeck dispelled the mythical kingdom of Prester John, that legendary Christian realm which medieval Europe so long believed to exist in mid-Asia. But Cathay was still a hidden land.

The first European penetration of the Chinese empire, as every reader knows, was due to those two Venetian merchants, the brothers Nicolo and Matteo Polo, and the former's famous son, Marco, the historiographer of their vast and varied wanderings. Actually the two elder Polos made two journeys to Far Cathay, one in 1260–69, the other in 1271–88. Upon this second expedition Nicolo took young Marco with him. For seventeen years they were in the service of Kubla Khan, the Mongol conqueror of China and lord of that "stately pleasure house" in Xanadu, "where Alph the sacred river ran down to a sunless sea." In 1293 the Polos returned to Europe, having gone out overland and come back by sea through the Straits of Sunda, the Indian Ocean, the Persian Gulf, and across Persia to Trebizond at the head of the Black Sea—the city built upon the mighty cliff whence Xenophon and the wearied Ten Thousand after perilous wanderings first descried the sea, and the glad cry, "Thalatta! thalatta!" burst from their lips. If there be any in this presence who have not yet read Marco Polo's *Travels*, let not Clio blush for shame.

The Roman church of the thirteenth century, in spite of its worldly and imperialistic policy, still was pervaded to some degree by the spirit of St. Francis. From the time of Plan-Carpini and Ruysbroeck the popes were interested in China as a promising field of missions. This interest was strengthened by the important consideration that Western Asia was becoming an increasingly difficult field of missionary labor owing to the growing inclination of the western Mongols toward Mohammedanism. In spite of heroic effort Christian missions failed among them.

Hence China became the greatest field of foreign missionary effort by the end of the thirteenth century because the Cross did not there have to compete with the Crescent, and our knowledge of the Far East and Cathay in the fourteenth and fifteenth centuries is much more due to ecclesiastical than secular informants. This history is at once a chapter in the history of medieval foreign missions and a chapter in the history of medieval exploration of the Far East.

In 1279 Bongrazio of Persiceto, having been elected general of the Franciscans, resolved to send an embassy to the Far East. Its chief was Brother John, born at Montecorvino (Poulia), who after having established the Persian mission had returned to Europe in 1283. Owing to the ease with which he learned the eastern languages and his indefatigable devotion, John of Montecorvino was actually the founder of the Far Eastern missions. Having got together a group of missionaries who received the papal blessing from Nicholas IV, he departed for the Orient in the very year of his return from Persia (1283).

After a sojourn in Armenia and Persia he went to India and at Malabar established a mission, the head of which was Friar Nicholas of Pistoia.

Thence he continued his journey by sea through the Straits of Sunda (Singapore) and at last arrived in China in 1298. The Grand Khan Kubla was then dead. His successor warmly welcomed the missionary, permitted him to preach where he pleased, and built a church for him adorned with an Italian campanile having three bells in it. John of Montecorvino learned the Chinese language, even to write it, and established a college for the education of young Chinese intending to be missionaries. He gathered together one hundred and fifty children, baptized them, and taught them Latin. He wrote for their use thirty-two psalters and breviaries. Some of these neophytes became able to recite the offices and to copy books for Catholic service.

The Chinese mission soon became important enough to require hierarchic organization. Thomas of Tolentino, chief of the Persian mission, was commissioned by John of Montecorvino to report to the pope the results which had been obtained. After a year of travel he found Clement V at Poitiers and in a solemn consistory the pope decided that John of Montecorvino should be made archbishop of Kambalik (Peking) with seven suffragans under his administration, and seven Friars Minor were immediately nominated to these distant sees. They left with letters from the pope, but most of them died en route. The survivors reached China in 1308. In 1312 a bull of Clement V named three new bishops in China, which raised the number of suffragans to ten. One of the most important of these bishoprics was that of Zayton (Touen-Tshaou-Fou, province of Fo-Kien), an important commercial port situated to the north of Canton, where in 1326 there was a colony of Genoese merchants. The Franciscans had been established there since 1308 and had erected three churches, a bath, and a warehouse for the western merchants. By 1314 there were in China fifty convents of the Friars Minor and they possessed, at the same time, a vicariate, Arabalek, located outside of the great wall of the Sacred Inner City.

The first archbishop of Peking, John of Montecorvino, died in 1330, having finished his work. When informed of his death in 1333, John XXII designated as his successor his brother Nicholas, then a reader in theology in the University of Paris, and permitted him to take with him twenty priests and six brothers. He sent with him letters to the Grand Khan and the chief princes of Asia.

The new archbishop did not arrive in China until 1338, four years after his nomination. So long was the interim that the Grand Khan had sent an embassy to the pope composed of sixteen persons under the lead of a Brother Andrew, and this depu-

tation arrived in Avignon in 1338 (at the very time
when the outward-bound mission had reached Peking). The pope, who at this time was Benedict
XII, in response to this Chinese embassy, sent
four apostolic legates to China chosen from among
the Friars Minor, and with them new letters for
the Grand Khan. In spite of the frightful distance
and difficulties of every kind, almost regular relations by this time had become established between
the popes and the Mongol rulers. The missions,
which failed to thrive in Mohammedan lands in
Western Asia, in China had a wonderful development.

The long journey of Brother Odoric of Pordenone shows us in a striking manner the condition
of the Christian missions in Asia in the first half
of the fourteenth century. Born in 1285 at Vil-
lanove near Pordenone (Friuli), Odoric entered at
the age of fifteen the monastery of the Franciscans
at Udine, and after some years was sent as a missionary to the Far East. He embarked at Venice
in 1304, tarried at Constantinople, took ship
thence to Trebizond, whence a march of ten days
brought him to Sultanyeh, via Erzaroum and
Tauris. In Persia he joined a caravan of Tartars
going to India, and traveled through Farsistan,
Irak, Kurdistan to Ormuz, where he took ship for
Malabar. Thence, after a tedious voyage through

the Straits he reached the port of Zayton in southern China where he found two houses of the Franciscans and a bishop, and deposited with them
some of the relics of the martyrs of India. He
visited Khan-Say (Han-Tshaou-Fou), situated on
a vast lagoon, which had been founded by the
missionaries of Zayton, and mentions in his *Nar-
rative* a Franciscan convent established at Yang-
Tchaou-Fou. At last Odoric reached Kambalik
(Peking). In 1330 Odoric returned to Europe, by
way of Thibet, twenty-six years after his departure, and reached Avignon again to render account
of his service to the pope. He was an old man and
had barely strength enough to get back to his home
monastery at Udine, where he died on January 14,
1331.

Again, in 1338 Benedict XII dispatched Giovanni de Marignolli on a mission to the Chinese
emperor. He was gone for fifteen years. His official *Relation* made to the pope is lost, but he became chaplain to the emperor Charles IV in 1354
and fortunately incorporated notes of his travels in
a chronicle of Bohemia which he wrote for the
emperor.

As late as 1353 Pope Innocent VI still received
at Avignon from the hand of Friar John of Florence
a letter sent by the Grand Khan in which the Mongol sovereign expressed his good feeling toward

Christianity. Once more the pope called for volunteers from among the Franciscans for the Far Eastern sees. The new missionaries were just about to leave when news of events in China suspended their departure. For in 1353 the terrible civil war which ended in 1368 with the overthrow of the Mongol dynasty by the Mings had broken out. The missions at Peking suffered fearfully, and some of the friars took refuge in the Kiptchak. In 1362 the fifth bishop of Zayton was put to death by the Mohammedans (who by now were aggressively proselyting in China). The new Ming dynasty abandoned Peking and transferred the capital to Nanking.

Nevertheless, in spite of these reverses, in 1370 Urban V organized a new mission and appointed Guillaume de Prato, a doctor of the University of Paris, to be archbishop of Peking. He went with twelve companions and was followed shortly afterward by seventy others. We know nothing as to the fate of these intrepid souls. But Christianity continued to survive in China for some years yet. For in 1391 an English friar named Roger and another, Ambrose of Siena, arrived in Europe from China to ask the pope for new missionaries.

While Europe's knowledge of Asia was thus substantially increased in the thirteenth and fourteenth centuries by these missionary friars and adventurous Italian merchants who went out by land and returned by sea around India—or reversed the course—the other great continent of Africa was not neglected. Medieval interest in Central Africa was keen, in spite of less success than the penetration of Asia. The fanaticism of the Mohammedans of the Maghreb—modern Algeria and Morocco—prevented penetration of Central Africa by Franciscan missionaries, as they penetrated Central Asia. But the Arabs were not so opposed to the conduct of trade. As early as the twelfth and thirteenth centuries Tripoli, Bona, Tenes, and Ceuta were regular ports of call for Genoese, Pisan, and Aragonese vessels. These places were termini of enormously long trade routes which the Arabs had broken across the Sahara as far as Lake Chad and the Niger River, where were situated the hitherto legendary cities of Ghana and Timbuktu, seat of the vast Negro Empire of the Hausa peoples, the most talented African race of history. They dwelt in mud-walled towns and were a cattle-raising and goat-herding people primarily; but they manufactured excellent textiles, dyed with local indigo, which was highly prized in the marts of the Mediterranean littoral. It was thus that the wild tale reached Europe told by thirteenth-century Arabs, of a race of black warriors who charged into battle mounted upon bulls, which was regarded as an invention on a par with the story of a pygmy race in Central Africa, until modern explorers verified both tales.

Historians have long hoped that evidence would some day be found to show that some adventurous merchant had made his way into the interior of Africa like another Marco Polo. This hope was realized in 1924 when M. Charles de la Roncière, curator of prints in the Bibliothèque Nationale and author of a remarkable history of the French marine, having for a time dropped his researches in French naval history and turned to the history of exploration and discovery during the Renaissance, found a letter written by one Antonio Malfante, directed to a Genoese named Giovanni Mariono, describing the country and peoples of the Niger, which he visited in 1447. But even Malfante had been anticipated. For, stimulated to further quest, M. de la Roncière unearthed earlier evidence of Central African exploration which gives to France the distinction, so far as we yet know, of having earliest penetrated the Dark Continent. This hero was Anselme Disalguier, a native of Toulouse, who sailed along the Senegalese and Guinea coasts in 1405 when Prince Henry the Navigator was still a youth, ascended the Niger River, and lived for eleven years in Gao, then the capital of the Songhay Empire. He returned to France in 1416, accompanied by a Negro wife, some mulatto children, a black physician of great skill, and some servants, to find France in the throes of war with England again, for it was the year after the disastrous battle of Agincourt. Unfortunately Disalguier, instead of writing his memoirs and preserving for us some account of the geography, peoples, and civilization of the Songhay Empire, busied himself with compiling a trilingual dictionary—French, Arabic, Negro—which has not survived, but of which we know from his letters.

Neither of these explorations seems to have made any impression on the cartography of the fifteenth century. Yet it is important to observe that the cosmographical school of the Jews of Majorca had more substantial knowledge of Central Africa than Europe was again to have until the time of Mungo Park and Bruce, late in the eighteenth century. In fact, European knowledge in this particular retrograded and forgot the lore which it had once learned. Columbian maps no longer know anything of the routes leading from the Mediterranean to Timbuktu, which are shown on the Catalan Atlas of Charles V of France (1364–80) or in the planisphere of Mecia de Viladestes (1413). Stranger still, concerning Asia its knowledge has lapsed as far back as the school of Alexandria. "Christopher Columbus' breviary for that part of the world is Ptolemy's *Cosmography*, published in Rome, 1478, of which one copy bears his signature." Yet Columbus possessed the Latin translation of Marco Polo's *Travels* printed at Antwerp in 1485. But he lacked faith in Marco Polo and complained that "not one of our contemporaries has been to the country of the Eastern Chinese."

The reason for this singular obscuration of geographical knowledge concerning Central and Farther Asia and interior Africa in the fifteenth century is to be found in the rise to national power and performance of the Atlantic seaboard states of Europe in this time—Portugal, Spain, France, England—an event which turned the front of Europe to the west. (The progress of the Ottoman Turkish conquests, as was long believed, were not responsible for this change.)

As the thirteenth and fourteenth centuries had been an epoch of exploration and discovery by land, so the fifteenth was a period of maritime discovery. In 1364 some adventurous merchants of Dieppe and Rouen, in whose veins one must believe the blood of the ancient vikings ran, and whose hearts were actuated by that same flair for adventure which made the Norsemen the discoverers of Iceland, Greenland, and America, coasted the Guinea coast and established a short-lived trade with the natives. But the renewal of the war with France by England ruined the continuation of the enterprise, although one finds survivals of French maritime discovery in the late fifteenth century. For in 1483 Louis XI sent an expedition to the Cape Verde Islands in search of turtle oil, which was reputed to be a cure for leprosy.

The glory of maritime discovery in the Atlantic fell to Portugal in the person of Prince Henry the Navigator (1394–1460), princely in title and more than princely in intelligence and character. A student of history, a passionate reader of voyages and travels, an accomplished cartographer, an expert seaman, Henry the Navigator for the first time brought the scientific knowledge of Europe to bear upon the problem of exploration and made it a business. Almost every year for thirty years he sent out ships to explore the west coast of Africa. In 1402 the Canary Islands were found. In 1418, Porto Santo was discovered; in 1419, the Madeira Islands; in 1441, Cape Blanco was rounded; in 1443, two of his captains passed Cape Bayador; in 1445, Cape Verde was discovered, and ten years later the islands of that name were lifted out of the sea; the exploration of Senegambia put an end to the belief of Europe that the equatorial zone was uninhabitable.

Portuguese traders and agriculturists were established in all these newly found places. Henry's death did not arrest the expansion of this little maritime kingdom. In 1477 the Azores were discovered. By 1484 the mouth of the Niger had been passed and that of the Congo discovered. Within the next three years these intrepid mariners had surveyed the coast of Angola, still a Portuguese possession, found the mouth of the Orange River, and —consummation of the dream of a century and more—Bartholomew Diaz in 1488 discovered the land's end of the Dark Continent so aptly named Cape of Good Hope. It remained for Vasco da Gama, greatest of all Portuguese captains, to crown the work; in 1498 he rounded the Cape, ran up the east coast of Africa through the channel between Madagascar and the mainland, discovered the Bay of Natal, which he so christened because he entered it on Christmas Day, Delagoa Bay, and Mombasa, now the great port of British East Africa, whence he set sail for Calicut. Vasco da Gama was the first European to burst into that vast sea, the Indian Ocean. The maritime route to the Far East was attained. The front of Europe was changed from the Mediterranean to the Atlantic. The achievement was of more immediate and greater importance than the discovery of America. For not until the rise of the Spanish Empire in the New World and the rival colonies of England, France, and Spain in North America in the seventeenth century, did the discovery of America attain a parity with that of the all-sea route to the Far East.

The heroism and dogged determination of these hardy Portuguese mariners is deserving of all praise. The Atlantic Ocean is notorious as the most formidable body of water upon the globe. When one examines models of the caravels then in use and knows their dimensions and tonnage, one marvels that these clumsy little ships ever survived. These craft had nothing to protect their hulks against the terrible terido, the tiny sea-worm which bored into their planking below water line, and which, in Richard Hakluyt's phrase, "many times pierceth and eateth through the strongest oak." Copper-bottoming of ships was still in the future. Again, in these long voyages of months and even of two years' duration, the ravages of scurvy were terrible. Moreover, there is probably no more inhospitable and dangerous coast in the world for the navigator than that of West Africa.

In addition to these adversities one must add the moral obstacles which had to be overcome. Superstitious fear was no less an inhibition than

physical obstacles. Sailors are proverbially a superstitious race and the heads of these Portuguese
crews were filled with vague and dreadful fears
born of the ignorance and credulity of the age.
"Why is the sun red at evening?" we read in a
medieval tract; "Because he looketh down into
hell." The common man in the Middle Ages believed that the earth was flat, and that the sun
renewed his fervent heat every night by going
down over the edge of the world into and through
hell, from which he emerged each morning. By actual observation these sailors knew that the farther
south they went the warmer the water became.
Therefore they prognosticated that if they continued to sail southward they ultimately would run
into seas of boiling hot water. We may not mini-
mize the effect of these and other like fears in retard-
ing the development of maritime exploration in
the fourteenth and fifteenth centuries.

What of Columbus? Is there new information
concerning him? Much. Romanticism, partisan
scholarship, and the ineradicable tendency of the
human mind to heroic glorification have, unfortunately for historical truth, distorted the nature and
significance of Columbus' achievements. Not by
elevating him above other men of his epoch, but by
intimately relating him to the men and movements
and ideas of his time may we truly understand him.

Recent historical research has increased our information above and beyond that contributed by those two self-expatriated American scholars, Henry Harrisse and Henry Vignaud. We owe this new information, as that concerning medieval African exploration, to M. de la Roncière.

The evidence is in a map which has been in possession of the Bibliothèque Nationale since 1849, labeled "Carte portugaise du XVI siècle," but which has hitherto escaped the attention of scholars.

This map displays the Mediterranean, the European seaboard, and the west coast of Africa, with the Azores, Canary, and Cape Verde Islands, as far south as the latitude of Angola. In addition there is a small map of the world after the Ptolemaic form, encircled by concentric celestial spheres. Arguing from the evidence afforded by the place-names upon this map M. de la Roncière is of the opinion that it was made between 1488 and 1492. The former date is indicated by details of the African coast which would have been unavailable before the voyage of Bartholomew Diaz in that year, while the latter date is justified by the absence of any indication of the New World. It is M. de la Roncière's truly astonishing contention that this map was actually made under Columbus' own direction and is the very map which he is known to have prepared in order to illustrate his designs, and to have presented to Ferdinand and Isabella at the time of his momentous interview with these sovereigns.

If this map is authentic and is what M. de la Roncière believes it to be, then we have new confirmatory evidence that Columbus was profoundly influenced by his reading of the *Imago mundi*, written at the beginning of the fifteenth century by Cardinal Pierre d'Ailly, for much of the rubrication on the map is verbally exact with the text of this book, which was printed at Louvain in 1483, and an example of this edition, copiously annotated in Columbus' handwriting, is one of the treasures of the Columbian Library in Seville.[1]

[1] The reader may find M. de la Roncière's account of the discovery of this map in *La carte de Christophe Colomb* ("The Map of Christopher Columbus"), text in French and English, each part consisting of forty-two columns of text, six figures in text, two plates, one large separate photographic facsimile (Paris: Edouard Champion, 1924). For important reviews of this work see Edward Heawood, *Geographical Journal*, LXV (1925), 247-51; G. E. Nunn, *Geographical Review*, XV (October, 1925); J. K. Wright, *Isis* VIII, (1925), 168-73, Gallois, *Annales de Géographie* (1925); Laloy, *Mercure de France* (February 1, 1925). Broadly speaking, European critics have accepted M. de la Roncière's contentions, while English and American critics have rejected them. Mr. Heawood thinks the map is "probably" of Columbian origin but regards the case as not proved; Mr. Nunn, on the other hand, bluntly says that "the map remains for the world no more than it was listed before M. de la Roncière gave it an undeserved notice, a portolan chart of the sixteenth century." M. de la Roncière has replied to these critics in *Isis*, VIII, 726-28.

Other new evidence concerning the career of Columbus has been brought to light by M. de la Roncière from the archives of Genoa which not only tends to confirm the tradition that Columbus was by birth a Genoese but, more, it provides us with new information. These documents disclose the fact that Columbus was for some time employed by the great Genoese mercantile firm of the Centurioni as a sugar-buyer in the Portuguese islands off of Africa—the Azores, Cape Verde, and Madeira Islands. These travels of Columbus were destined to have a momentous consequence, for he was thereby brought into intimate contact with many Portuguese and Spanish merchants, captains, and navigators, whose talk stimulated his curiosity and aroused his interest in certain Western Islands and the possibility of reaching the East by sailing westward around the globe.

These Western Islands were not Newfoundland, which Bristol seamen had been looking for ever since 1480 in the ocean to the west of Ireland and which Portuguese navigators certainly had found by 1489,[1] but another great island or islands known as Antillia. The new information was not

[1] Columbus had learned of this discovery of Newfoundland from his brother. It was to safeguard the rights of Portugal to the mysterious seven cities of fabulous wealth believed to be in Newfoundland that Pope Alexander VI drew the famous line of demarcation of the globe in 1493.

mythical and vague but concrete. This information had been picked up by a Spanish captain,
Martin Alonzo Pinzon, and was positive to the
effect that some Portuguese seamen had, about ten
years before, discovered a great island, again having "seven cities," far west of the Madeiras and
Azores, and that the pope had been informed of the
discovery. Forthwith Pinzon went to Rome—this
was in 1491—where, in the Vatican Library, he
documented himself with a book and a map which
confirmed the rumor that he had picked up.[1] The
book was Pierre d'Ailly's *Imago mundi*, which Pinzon first brought to Columbus' attention. But of
far greater significance to history was this map.

Columbus' first great inspirer had been his
brother, Bartholomew, contact with whom was lost
when the latter entered the French naval service.
The second—and greater—was Martin Alonzo
Pinzon. It is no detraction of Columbus to say
that Pinzon deserves equal merit with Columbus
for the event in 1492.

Martin Alonzo Pinzon was the captain of the
Pinta, one of the three caravels in which Columbus
sailed from Palos on August 3, 1492. Columbus
had a double idea in his mind: he was in quest of

[1] Roncière, *La carte de Christophe Colombe*, cols. 30–31; testimony
of Francisco Garcia, a sailor on the Pinta, and Martin Alonzo Pinzon's
son, made October 1, 1515. See *Los Pleitos de Colon* (ed. Fernandez
Duro Madrid, 1894), II, 217, 228.

an island, less fabulous than heretofore, yet mysterious; and he believed in the existence of a shorter route to the Indies than the Red Sea route or the African periplus. But Pinzon was the more practical-minded of the two. For Columbus was still so vague in his mind that he sailed almost due west for two months after stopping at the Canaries, to the disquietude of Pinzon, who on October 6 signaled for a change of course more toward the southwest, as Columbus' log book records. Five days later land was sighted.

It is manifest, from a critical study of this new evidence, that we must revise the current story of the momentous discovery in 1492. Columbus appears as vague and unpractical when compared with his great captain, and withal, a poorer navigator. Columbus had the good fortune to secure the financial backing of Ferdinand and Isabella, but he was more the organizer of the expedition than the brains of the expedition. High honor—if not the greater honor—must be given to Martin Alonzo Pinzon. It was Pinzon who revealed to Columbus the map on which the discovery of a new continent depended. In the words of M. de la Roncière: "On this map, doubtless, the fate of the world was decided." The "new chart," which Columbus tells us in his log book he intended to make, implies a previous map, which could have been none other than a copy of the one found by Pinzon in the Vatican Library. For Columbus again in the log book (September 25) records that he consulted a map belonging to Pinzon, on which "certain islands were painted."

But there are other—and too neglected as-pects—of the history of the age of discovery to which I would direct your attention. They are these: first, that European discovery and explora-tion in the fourteenth and fifteenth centuries owed an incalculable debt to the services of Arabic ex-ploration, cartography, and science in the Middle Ages; second, without the progress of Europe in mathematics during these centuries and the ad-vance in technical skill which enabled these voy-agers to be provided with new and reasonably ac-curate instruments of navigation it would have been well-nigh impossible for these distant voyages to have been made; third, shipbuilding was much improved.

The Arabs not only preserved the scientific knowledge of the Greeks; they enlarged and cor-rected it. The khalif Al-Mamoun translated the works of Ptolemy the geographer, and himself measured an arc of the meridian. The experiment is described by Abul-Feda and by Ibn Youmis, and confirmed the researches of Erastothenes. The as-tronomer Abul-Hasan determined the latitude and longitude of 135 positions in Spain and North Africa. He far exceeded Ptolemy in the accuracy of his calculations. For example, his greatest error in longitude is 4 degrees and 12 minutes, whereas Ptolemy made one of 18 degrees. His determination of the length of the Mediterranean was exact within 52 minutes, while Ptolemy made an error of 19 degrees. Similar tables were made for Asia clear to China by Nacir-ed-din, a protégé of Hulagu, the grandson of Ghenghiz Khan, and were revised by Ulu, prince of Sogdiana, in the fifteenth century. The latitude of Samarkand was determined exactly, though the longitude erred by 13 degrees. It was always more difficult to calculate longitude than latitude on account of lack of a device to measure time with absolute accuracy. The meridian of Baghdad was established. The latitude of the astronomical observatory of Maraghah was rigorously exact, but the longitude was in error by 6 degrees, 38 minutes with reference to the meridian of Baghdad.

Mohammedan sway in the Middle Ages was the widest in the world, for it extended from Spain to Canton. It is worth observing in connection with this tremendous expansion of Mohammedan power that the Arabic geographers had a very large amount of source material to draw upon. In the first place they had pilot books, travel records, relations of campaigns, merchant and pilgrim accounts. In the second place they drew upon Egyptian, Coptic, Greek, and Persian sources. The navigators themselves were indebted to previous civilizations for much of their knowledge of navigation. The geographer Idrisi writes, "The captain used to sit in the poop of the vessel furnished with numerous and useful instruments," among which was certainly the astrolabe and the sounding lead, and perhaps the compass.

There is a very large literature written by Mohammedan travelers and geographers pertaining to this Indian, African, and Chinese trade of the Arabs. The *Sinbad Saga* is based on the narratives of "the two Mussulman travellers" and similar records, such as those of Misar-al-Dolaf, who in 942 went to China, supplemented by Greek myths and traditions of Alexander the Great, Indian tales, and Persian lore. It is an oriental form of Europe's *Wondrous Adventures of Sir John Mandeville*. Sinbad's localities have been identified as Japan(?), China, Borneo, Sumatra, Ceylon, the Coromandel coast, and Madagascar(?). In the ninth century Ibn-Khordabeh described India, Ceylon, the East Indies, Khan-Fu in China, the mouths of the Yangtze and Hoang-Ho rivers, and seems to have had information about Korea and Japan, probably from Chinese merchants. Ibn-

Haukel in the same century knew Africa and India but not the Far East. The same is true of Macoudi in the tenth century; he knew Persia, India, Ceylon, Central Asia from Ferghana to the Caspian, North Africa, and Spain but not the Straits or China. In the twelfth century the great Arabian geographer, Idrisi, having traveled widely and studied much, settled down at the court of Roger II at Palermo and compiled a valuable geography of the known Arab world.

That European cartographers went to school to Arabic cartographers is manifested by the portolans, or hand maps, carried by navigators, and by the maps of the world designed in this age. That of Marino Sanudo was made in 1321; the Catalan *mappemonde* was drawn in 1375; that of Fra Mauro was painted on the walls of the monastery of San Michele near Venice, probably in 1459. They attest the progress made in geographical knowledge during the Renaissance. North Africa as far as Timbuktu and Melli are outlined on the Catalan map. The map of Fra Mauro shows an exact knowledge of Abyssinia. The portolans exceeded the mappemondes in accuracy, for they were used by practical navigators. We possess many of the fourteenth and fifteenth centuries. The maritime republics of Italy, Venice, and Genoa, and the island of Majorca, a dependency of the kingdom of Aragon, which from the earliest page of its history was deeply interested in the Mediterranean and African trade, were the chief places of production of the portolans, which the Castilian and Portuguese navigators later borrowed and improved upon. The accuracy of some of these portolans is astonishing. For example, no map of the Black Sea was so good as they until the Russian survey of 1816.

In the course of time European mathematicians worked out fuller and more accurate tables of latitude and longitude than any devised by Arabic scholars. There is no more striking illustration of the practical value of purely scientific researches—which the man in the street in his ignorance contemns—than the indebtedness of European discovery and exploration to the progress in mathematics made during the Renaissance. Here again the root is a long one. For it goes back to Albertus Magnus in the thirteenth century. It is also an impressive fact that Renaissance mathematics owed almost all its progress to German mathematicians. There is no great Italian mathematician between Leonard of Pisa in the thirteenth century and Jerome Cardanus in the sixteenth.

The continuity of German medieval and Renaissance mathematical thought is very striking. Beginning with Albertus Magnus the line runs through Jordan of Saxony, Conrad of Megenburg, Nicholas of Cusa, George Peuerbach, Regiomontanus (or Johannes Müller of Königsberg, 1436–76), and the two Germanized Poles, Albertus Brudzewski (1445–97) and Copernicus (1473–1543). Albertus Magnus taught Jordan of Saxony. Peuerbach was the master of Regiomontanus, to whom Copernicus was deeply indebted. Nicholas of Cusa (who died in 1464) anticipated the Copernican theory of a heliocentric universe by declaring that whatever the earth might do, he was sure that Mercury and Venus revolved around the sun.

In this galaxy of famous mathematicians, Regiomontanus has special interest for us. His *Tables*, published in 1475, were important both for astronomy and for the voyages of discovery. These *Tables* covered the period from 1473 to 1560, and gave sines for each minute of arc, longitudes for sun and moon, latitude for the moon, and a list of predicted eclipses from 1475 to 1530. They became the handbook of progressive navigators in the late fifteenth century. Although America had not yet been discovered, Regiomontanus, like every educated man in the Middle Ages, knew that the earth was a sphere—for the belief that the earth was flat was merely vulgar opinion—and though he knew not whether land or water, whether continents or seas, lay on the other side of the globe, nevertheless he calculated meridians and lines of latitude for the complete circle.

But Columbus navigated according to a chart like that in Paris, ungraduated in latitude and longitude. In so doing, he was not up to date. For Martin Behaim's globe of 1492 "represents the whole size of the world, as well in longitude as in latitude, measured geometrically according to Ptolemy and according to the knight Marco Polo." Thus Columbus was adhering to the practice in the Portuguese and Spanish navies of using ungraduated portolans in conjunction with manuals in which latitudes and longitudes were given. But Columbus' intention was to make a new map in which, to use his own words, "I shall represent in painting the figuration of the whole latitude from the equinoctial line, and of the longitude from the Occident." It cannot be proved, but apparently either Columbus or Pinzon possessed a copy of Regiomontanus' *Tables*, and we know that this was so in the cases of Vespucci, Vasco da Gama, and Magellan. If Columbus had been able to calculate his longitude as accurately as his latitude he would not have confused the West India Islands with the East Indies in 1492. For their latitude and longitude were known from Arabic geographers. But the calculation of longitude was always a very difficult matter, owing to lack of accurate time pieces, until the eighteenth century. La Salle missed the mouth of the Mississippi by more than four hundred miles in the seventeenth century.

As for the compass, though it had been known since the ninth century, it was not of use in navigation—at least in Europe—until the Renaissance. It emancipated vessels from being compelled to keep in sight of the coast, and without it, it would have been impossible to have penetrated the Atlantic. It was a sufficiently accurate instrument in the temperate and equatorial zones, but the magnetic pole seriously deranged it in those heroic and disastrous voyages which endeavored to discover the fabulous North West passage to China.

But the sands in the imaginary hourglass upon my desk have already run their course and my time has expired. Too long, perhaps, I have trespassed upon your patience and your generous attention.

The discovery movement of the Renaissance had its roots deep down in European history. It was a part of the general awakening of Europe in the fourteenth and fifteenth centuries. It was not of one nation, but of many nations. It was a religious, a commercial, a political, and a scientific movement. It revolutionized European circumstances. It revolutionized ideas. It was the expression of a tremendous amount of energy, and no less the expression of an impressive amount of the nobleness of human character. Honor to those who traversed strange lands under enormous physical and moral difficulties; who faced privation and famine, the hot glare of deserts, the desolation of sparse plateaus peopled by savage men, the blizzards of the highest mountains on the planet. And honor, too, to those as bold sailors and navigators who went down to the vasty deep of the stormy Atlantic in ships which were mere shallops; who encountered hurricane and typhoon and treacherous currents, reefs, and rocks; who endured exile and scurvy, many of whom never came back to tell the tale of their exploits.

THE SOCIETY OF THE ITALIAN
RENAISSANCE

THE SOCIETY OF THE ITALIAN
RENAISSANCE

FERDINAND SCHEVILL

IF WE could call the society of the Italian Renaissance back to life and give ourselves the pleasure of exploring it at our ease, it might well be that we would presently exclaim, how like ourselves! and immediately after, with equal justification and conviction, how unlike! For glancing first at the individual units, the men and women constituting the Renaissance group, they would be found to be wrestling, much like ourselves, with the eternally identical problem of living, and consequently to be swayed in their daily lives by the same hopes, despairs, suspicions, hates, and loves. It is our human emotions which chiefly lend color to existence, and they were the same then as now. In fact they have changed little since the far days when Agamemnon was lord in Argolis; and it is this persistence which explains why we can follow with understanding and sympathy not only King Agamemnon's tribulations before windy Troy but also the agitations besetting all the subsequent generations of our kind all the way down to the contemporary problems of our own admired King Henry of Detroit.

Even the society of the Italian Renaissance, as distinct from its component units, would be found, if we could revisit it, to be organized on lines broadly similar to our own. We would observe a great body of country-dwellers, living by agriculture, marked off from a less numerous but more concentrated mass of city-dwellers, living by manufacture and exchange. Within the cities there would be discovered our own main occupational groups: merchants, bankers, shopkeepers, craftsmen, representatives of the professions, common laborers. Everything about the revisited town, its winding streets, its fountains and houses, would indeed seem quaint and rudimentary and, not least of all so, the massive circumambient wall, but we would not fail to recognize the family resemblance which this urban progenitor bears, even in the matter of outward appearance, to the modern offspring of our immediate acquaintance.

But even as we noted these various resemblances, our attention would be vigorously assaulted by astounding differences. And when our bewilderment at last clarified, we would indubitably summarize our impressions in a single word: the machine. The machine was absent in the Italian Renaissance and everything was absent that goes with it by way of factory and mass production. By the same token there were lacking also the railroad, the steamboat, and those still more revolutionary means of communication, the telegraph and the telephone, not to mention the most recent acceleration signified by the aeroplane and the radio. Without doubt we, the imaginary visitors of the Renaissance town, would be so struck by these absences that we would be tempted to exaggerate them. It is our habit to swell with pride over our innumerable inventions and to pity our poor simpletons of ancestors who lived their dull and colorless lives without them. And yet, I would submit, the resemblances and identities between those Italian townsmen and ourselves are at least as important as the differences. They serve, above all, to put us in intimate touch with the past and to convince us that the life we are leading today has flowed on uninterruptedly ever since the time the Venetians first took to the sea and the Florentines achieved for their town the dangerous eminence of the leading textile center of the world.

Let me give my thought touching these matters a summary form: the human identities from age to age are invaluable as conveying the assurance of the continuity of life and history, while the differences represent new births testifying to the inexhaustible creativeness of the human spirit. And, therefore, although I have just celebrated continuity, let it not be said that I make light of change. Quite properly and normally, after all, the historian singles it out in his analysis of life, for by the factor of change, defining the novel contribution, he appraises the creative activity of each new generation of men. And if we consider well, is not that what all history is about, the recovery of the particular contribution made by each past age? Is not that, specifically, what the history of the Italian Renaissance is about? At least I shall assume that having requested me to discuss the social aspect of the Italian Renaissance, you will want to know what that society brought to light that was new, fresh, and significant. In short, our story tonight will be essentially a story of social change.

The society of the Renaissance evolved very gradually out of an earlier society that we may describe summarily as feudal and medieval. Feudal society was based on the manor; was overwhelmingly agricultural; and, as unimaginably rude and simple, boasted by way of trade little other than the primitive and local variety known as barter. Into this society, around the year 1000, was projected the town; and the town as concerned with trade and the crafts was a foreign element in the manorial system and precipitated a revolutionary ferment. For several hundred years the town sought to gain a footing within established feudal society and gradually succeeded, though not without progressively breaking the dominant system to pieces. The centuries after the tenth are full of this conflict between town and country, that is, between two ways of living, and bear witness to the slow disentanglement of the new urban units from the smothering arms of feudalism. For reasons of geography, which any map of medieval Europe will make clear, the town movement was more potent in Italy than in any other country of Europe. In Italy, too, the emancipation of the town from feudal control came earliest and was most complete. Agrarian supremacy may in fact be said to have been broken before the close of the thirteenth century. If we agree that the Renaissance is the period *after* the thirteenth century, the period approximately, let us say, from 1300 to 1530, we are faced, by way of clarifying our purpose, with the obligation of giving this chronological division a preliminary characterization. And we need not hesitate for a moment. The Italian Renaissance is the period of the liberated towns, when the interest centers, on the one hand, in their social-political organization, and, on the other, in their cultural achievements. One of these developments cannot be understood without the other; and if, in accordance with the plan of this lecture series, I am going to limit myself strictly to the social field, it is with the hope that my exposition will serve to facilitate your approach to the marvelous self-expression of the period revealed in the fine arts.

Confronted with the problem of the urban situation during the Renaissance we are, on looking close, at once struck by the fact that only the northern half of the peninsula may be fairly considered urban. The southern half, including Rome and its immediate territory together with the kingdom of Naples, was never greatly affected by the communal movement and remained preponderantly feudal. The result is that Italy in the Renaissance was, socially considered, not one but two, a revolutionary urban north confronted by a conservative agrarian south, and that the disparity between them became an important cause of much secret and open friction in the peninsula. If the north, comprising the Lombard plain, the Genoese and Venetian seaboards, and the province of Tuscany became a mighty city area, it was due to the simple geographic fact that this section, possessed of an easy access to the Mediterranean Sea and lying at the same time within hail of the passes of the Alps, was ideally located for the importation and distribution over Europe of the highly prized goods of the east. This Levantine trade, made up, as everybody knows, of spices, silks, jewels, ivory, and other luxury articles of relatively slight bulk, constituted the economic basis of the Italian towns, and they greedily and successfully monopolized it until the discoveries of the Portuguese, by opening up the Atlantic route to the oriental treasure-house, dropped the curtain on Italian prosperity.

But we are not here concerned with the Italian twilight. It is high-noon in Italy during the Renaissance; but this high-noon, I ask you to note, was limited to the Italian north. Without any doubt a few southern cities such as Rome, the seat of the papacy, and Naples, the capital of the kingdom of that name, were sympathetically stirred by the northern movement. In the main we may think of them as isolated points shining by reflected light in wide regions over which feudalism continued to suspend an unbroken pall.

It is therefore only northern Italy with which we are concerned, and this north was during the Renaissance thickly strewn with towns or, as the Italians say, *comuni*. The trade which was their life had been gathering strength for several centuries and during the period under consideration reached its height. From the start trade was a voluntary activity engaged in by courageous, self-reliant individuals, and produced, in furtherance of its successful prosecution, the famous volun-

tary groups called gilds. Next to the family, the
gild, which pursued as its immediate end the purpose of welding together for protection men following the same occupation, became the most important germ-plasm of the commune. If the gilds of
merchants came first in time, they were almost immediately followed by the gilds of craftsmen; and
both classes of gilds tended to become more numerous and diversified as the town grew prosperous and waxed in size. The two kinds of gilds, merchant gilds and craft gilds, clearly proclaimed that
the town lived by production and exchange, and
that gilds and towns alike owed their existence to
an economic impulse. This should be clearly recognized, though the fundamentally economic
character of the gilds must not blind us to the
fact, that, enormously vital and responsive to
their opportunities, they took on also a social, a
religious, and, in many instances, a political character.

The central economic kernel of the gild, its life
principle as it were, was the monopoly of the local
market. This monopoly was supposed to bring advantage to all the adherents of a particular gild,
but in reality it profited only the full-fledged members, who were called masters. These masters exercised tremendous powers. They determined the
quality and price of the manufactured article, fixed

the wages to be paid helpers or journeymen, and laid down the rules under which apprentices were to be received and governed. By virtue of these prerogatives they achieved a most distinguished social status, which was reflected in their dress and bearing and in the honors publicly accorded them. In this way the gilds, economic institutions though they pre-eminently were, came to fill a large place in the social order. Further, in view of the age in which they originated, they became inevitably steeped in the medieval religious spirit. Each gild acquired and handsomely furnished a chapel for the celebration of religious services; it chose a patron saint to whose protection it commended its affairs; and it exercised toward its members, overtaken by misfortune and, particularly, toward the widows and orphans of members, those offices of charity which are the essence of practical Christianity.

So long as the town was young and absorbed by the struggle with feudalism, that is, throughout the period antecedent to the Renaissance, there was a substantial equality among the gilds and a certain vigorous democracy obtained binding together the whole body of the citizens. No sooner, however, did the town by defeating its feudal oppressors acquire a comparative security than the democratic spirit weakened and the ancient and familiar chasm opened between rich and poor. Wealth, and in some instances great wealth, was won by particularly capable members of the trading gilds quick to take advantage of the opportunities offered by a changing world. These prosperous gildsmen will be found in probably every instance to have engaged in business on a more than local scale and thus to have broken through the original narrow purpose of the gild. This institution, we have seen, was planned for the individual town at a time when, just beginning to raise its head, the town thought of itself as a self-sufficient economic unit. But the moment trade expanded, the moment it became national and international in scope, the gild, though perhaps still a help to the retailer, "to the butcher, the baker, and candlestick-maker," loomed as a sore hindrance to the ambitious wholesaler. We are here touching on that phase in the development of Italian economic life marked by the advent of the merchant adventurer or merchant prince operating with an accumulation of free capital. These large-scale merchants were the men who built up the vast commerce of Venice and Genoa with the Levant, concentrated the trade of the Po valley in Milan, and made Florence the industrial center of the Mediterranean world. And whenever a lesser town of Tuscany or Lombardy shared in the economic expansion it was due to a similar group of enterprising agents in its midst.

We may sum up this economic movement by saying that the Renaissance saw the birth of capitalism and witnessed the first bid made by capitalists since the passing of the Roman Empire to dominate production and exchange. It followed that combinations of capitalists in the form of banks and stock companies became more powerful than gilds and, before long, undertook to act in all but complete disregard of them. The gilds therefore declined in importance though they by no means disappeared. Indeed to the very close of our period they will be found in all Italian cities, exercising a varying measure of influence but rarely, if ever, continuing in control of the economic situation. More particularly in all the leading towns, where the concentration of wealth was most manifest, the economic emphasis shifted definitely from the gilds to the capitalists. That means that the widening of the local market to European dimensions, which is the outstanding economic phenomenon of the age, brought with it the irresistible triumph of large-scale enterprise. To give the movement a convenient label call it, if you will, capitalism; but do not forget that capitalism has an ethical and psychological side and that, viewed from this angle, it presents itself as individualism.

The Renaissance has been frequently and properly identified with individualism, but it has not often enough been pointed out that the new individual assertiveness first manifested itself in the economic realm.

With rich men, merchants and bankers, towering over their fellow-citizens, what followed as a political consequence? The gild régime in its origin carried with it enough economic equality to produce a drift toward a democratic system of government. True, democracy was rarely if ever achieved; but though only operative as an ideal, it communicated an appreciable general vitality to the towns in their first period. However, as soon as rich men appeared commanding extensive resources, they were moved to acquire a measure of political power corresponding to their economic domination; and this ambition necessarily clashed with the resolution of their humbler fellow-citizens not only to hold fast to the political rights already won but, if possible, to increase them. The result was a civil struggle which was not decided for some generations and in which the democracy uniformly went to the wall. Moreover, except in some few instances, of which Venice is the most notable, the oligarchs proved to be the losers also. As is usual enough in periods of prolonged domestic disturbance the victory was won by a third party, an

outsider who interposed himself between the com-
batants. This is the military dictator. The Italians
refer to him as the *condottiere;* and when he man-
aged to establish himself in office with some degree
of permanence they call him prince or despot.

Now the condottiere, or prince, is, as is well
known, the leading political figure of the Italian
Renaissance. As soon as he gains a footing in a
town, he usurps political authority and then attempts to persuade both warring factions, oligarchs and democrats, to accept his rule in return
for the benefits of a general peace which he imposes
by means of his soldiers. It is not usually his plan
to favor one group against the other, since the best
chance for prolonging his control plainly lies in his
striking a balance between the opposing parties.
However, he soon discovers that the economic welfare of the town depends chiefly on the great merchants; or, if he is slow to learn this lesson, they,
as alert and intelligent business men enjoying an
enviable social status, are sure to seize an early
opportunity to bring the fact to his attention. In
case they should, in an access of alarm, go the
length of transferring their enterprises to another
town, the princely revenues would quickly be so
disastrously reduced that the emigrants would be
almost certain to be recalled on their own terms.
By reason of these considerations the new despotic

sovereign usually ends by identifying himself with the great merchants; and the political revolution which concludes the struggle between oligarchy and democracy may without hesitation be declared to signify, on the economic side, a victory for capitalism.

But our analysis of the despotic régime may not rest here. The military dictator came to the Italian town because there was no other way out; and therefore, in spite of much democratic lamentation of a doctrinaire order, he represented an undoubted political advance. This is easily demonstrable, for, taking the new rulers by and large, they at once and energetically attacked the problem of giving the town a government better adapted to its needs than the more or less republican régime which had gone by the boards. The first care of the despot was to establish police and courts calculated to give security to persons and property. Then he provided for water, paving, bridges, and public hygiene. As the taxes could not for a moment be neglected, he reorganized and unified them, providing at the same time for an efficient service of trained officials. Finally, he created heads of departments, with the title of secretaries, whom he kept around his person and who, constituting the prince's court, were in effect the central government. So grave were the difficulties besetting the new sovereign, who, we must always remember, had the hazardous status of a usurper, that unless he faced his task with creative intelligence and brought the government to a higher measure of efficiency than it had been able to attain under the older democratic system, he was lost. His goal was success; and success imperatively demanded that he be active, inventive, and free from the bondage of tradition. The prince and his court are in the fullest sense of the word new men, *novi homines*, and constitute the exact equivalent in politics of the great merchants in the field of economics. And exactly like the merchants, they represent the victory of that moral attitude which is currently called individualism and which is the pervasive atmosphere of the Renaissance.

Engaged upon a social survey of the Renaissance, we are now prepared to say that its special genius seemed to be to bring to birth novel and highly individualized groups. Anything more individualized than the merchant adventurers, who were the first capitalists, it is hard to imagine, unless it be the princes and their officials, who made up the new governing class. But we are not at the end of the creations of this age. The merchants, spinning new threads from east to west and north to south over the known world, the rulers, replacing outworn forms of government with more practicable devices, gradually produced or helped to produce an intellectual revolution. You are all familiar with it under the name of humanism. Like every intellectual revolution humanism is a revaluation of experience. More particularly, it challenged the meaning attached to existence by the theological leaders of the Middle Age and declared, timidly at first and then more boldly, in favor of interpreting life in purely mundane or human terms. This was tantamount to affirming that existence was less a divine and predetermined than a haphazard and secular affair; and as the ancients had upheld the same position, the humanists, in support of their bold contention, appealed naturally and with fervor to the authority of the Greeks and Latins. From the angle of this appeal humanism took on the appearance of a revival of antiquity, and as such it has been not improperly celebrated, though often with a too exclusive emphasis. For, while conceding that there was such a revival and that it is highly important philologically and philosophically, it is *historically* much more significant that a group of thinkers arose who challenged the contempt with which the medieval theologians regarded this world of ours and who affirmed unequivocally that the earth was a goodly habitation and our individual existence a most precious gift. The humanists are therefore intellectual rebels on a social par with the great merchants and the usurping princes. All three are strictly Renaissance groups and each re-enforces the other. Let us agree that many humanists, Petrarch for example, will be found to equivocate, planting themselves with one foot in the Middle Age and with the other in the Renaissance. Such compromises are so common in periods of intellectual movement that they may be accepted as normal. After a few decades the humanistic successors of Petrarch divested themselves and often with radical completeness of their medieval heritage. Considered in the mass, the intellectuals, beginning with Petrarch, may be regarded as a group of innovators, who, breaking down the mental barriers hemming in the medieval outlook, declared for freedom of thought and of investigation. They are consequently a characteristic expression of the dominant individualism of the age.

The fourth and last social group impregnated with the Renaissance ferment is in the eyes of the world at large the most important of all, the artists. Not that there had been no artists in the early towns still dominated by gild democracy. Truth to tell, west-European art first came into vigorous existence in the gild period and, following the universal trend, its practitioners formed associations for mutual aid and protection. That life in that early urban age was very simple is shown by the circumstance that ordinary stonecutters were not distinguished from architects and sculptors, and that all these workers alike were embraced in the identical gild of masons. As to the gild of painters, the early documents show that the artists of the brush were chiefly occupied with such household matters as painting coats of arms on shields and decorating the wedding chests, called *cassoni*, so characteristic of the period. Even when, with the rather shadowy Cimabue, fresco-painting came into fashion and art mounted to a higher level, the painter worked so contentedly under the guidance of the all powerful Church that all his productions remained steeped in the medieval spirit.

The spirit of rebellion, which is the Renaissance, no sooner reached the artists than the old patriarchal conditions dissolved like mist before the rising sun. It is a pleasure reserved to the close followers of the artistic movement to assemble the multitudinous evidences of the transition from the medieval to the Renaissance level of expression. We are not here concerned with this transition farther than to note its general trend. And ought we to be surprised that, quite like the other revolutionary groups, the public officials, the merchant-princes, and the humanists, the awakened artists, too, planted their feet on this solid earth and joyfully sang its praises? To be sure they did not on this account abandon the religious themes which had been the early inspiration of their art. But how different the spirit in which they now presented them! The scenes from the life of Jesus and his mother, the earthly pilgrimage of Holy Fathers like St. Augustine, or the moving exploits of more recent saints like Francis of Assisi were thrown into the realm of everyday experience and given, if anything, an added poignancy by being brought closer to the human heart. By the witness of a long line of noble fifteenth century painters theology is in retreat during the Renaissance, while humanism advances until the courageous painters penetrate successively all the veils with which their vision had been hampered and they are enabled with liberated and amazed eyes to gaze upon the golden prospect of our earth. Arrived at this point, they, who had been occupied hitherto exclusively with religious subjects, cultivated novel secular fields as well and brought to a high perfection portraiture, landscape, and those scenes of everyday life in town and country commonly comprised under the name of genre. In short, all of existence, not merely the religious segment of it, became the province of the painter.

And the refreshing breath which is upon the painter falls also on the architect and sculptor.

The work of each now becomes differentiated from that of the other and both become disentangled from the mason, whom they leave behind in the more congenial company of his brother-craftsmen, the carpenters, cobblers, tailors. Look around first among the sculptors. They work in the same spirit as the painters and seek their inspiration in the multiple forms of mother nature. For confirmation fasten more closely on the work of a single sculptor like Donatello. Actual living children are no fresher than those fashioned by his hands, actual youths no more vigorous or winning. Though Donatello patently sought his inspiration in the world about him, it is not too much to say that by gracing his realism with a touch of magic he did not imitate, he transcended nature. And note besides, that if the Florentine sculptor's figures hymn the joy of living, he is not estranged from his religious heritage, as that last embodiment of the medieval dream of knighthood, the noble St. George of Or San Michele, convincingly testifies. The Renaissance, at least as represented by the particular sculptor under review, carries the past with it on its onward march toward the future.

And if we turn to the architects, what an opportunity opened to them in this expanding age! The towns grew so rapidly that they had to be rebuilt and the walls pulled down to be re-erected on an outer line tracing a more generous circumference. There were public buildings to be raised for the new government, palaces and villas for the new rich, while the need of churches may have declined as compared with the high Middle Age, but nevertheless continued active in a society still devoted to its faith so far as the masses of the people were concerned. Though Florence, Venice, Siena, Bologna, and their neighbors have experienced later transformations, especially in the most recent generations through the coming of the factory and the railroad, what still chiefly appeals to us about them as town entities and lends them individual distinction in our eyes is the stamp the Renaissance architect has left upon them.

Let us now mount an eminence, as it were, and send a sweeping glance over this society chiefly with a view to taking in, in a summary way, the social changes effected between the beginning and the end of the period. For the swarming peasants, the hardy tillers of the soil, little has been changed. With the weakening of feudalism some of the worst features of serfdom have disappeared, but in the main the agricultural workers carry the same yoke and live in the same straitened circumstances as before. The identical statement holds for the lower elements of the urban population: they have become more numerous with the growth of the towns, but neither economically nor politically are they able to make themselves heard. The significant social changes have all occurred in the upper levels of the town, to which belong the princes and their courts, the great merchants, the intellectuals called humanists, and the artists. These four groups are a new birth, resulting from a revolution in which the medieval barriers have been broken down and the path has been cleared for individual talent. The Middle Age was a strictly associative period; the Renaissance, at least for the upper urban groups which principally set their imprint on the age, was emphatically individualistic. This signifies that the princes, merchants, humanists, and artists felt themselves largely liberated from the bondage of tradition and responded to the powerful and characteristic urge to achieve the fullest possible measure of self-realization.

If I offer these conclusions as the comprehensive social formula of the Renaissance, you will, before accepting it, want to know whether the Renaissance saw itself in these terms and in this specific light. Most emphatically it did. Conceding that it was not in possession of our modern terminology and that consequently it did not have much to say about individualism or self-realization, it nonetheless worshiped the ends implied in these concepts under another name, that of *virtù*.

Virtù is the activating ideal familiar to the time. It is in everybody's mouth and heart, and although it is etymologically identical with our English word "virtue," it carries so little of the current moral connotation of virtue as to be more nearly its opposite. Virtù required of its followers that life be led strenuously with a view to the highest personal achievement and sustained by a heart whose beat never weakened. Failure was conceivable under the press of adverse circumstances but not irresolution or cowardice. It goes without saying that a striving so inflamed and concentrated was incompatible with a scrupulous regard for the rules of behavior obtaining in a well-ordered society, and as a matter of fact the worshiper of virtù treated established rules with a lofty indifference. His concern, his single concern, was with himself and his chosen work, which to bring to a triumphant conclusion he was prepared to be absolutely ruthless. Virtue, as we have come to interpret the word, inculcates a code of conduct dictated by individual submission to the general welfare; the virtù of the Renaissance Italian is personal grandeur achieved, if necessary, by trampling the world under foot. A virtù of this order may without hesitation be identified with what the living generation would call rampant individualism.

To clinch the argument let us briefly examine

two literary works, which, as brilliant embodiments of the ideal of virtù, are among the most famous and, in certain prudish eyes, undoubtedly the most infamous productions of the period. I refer to Machiavelli's *Prince* and to Benvenuto Cellini's *Autobiography*. Machiavelli was the most acute observer of his day of the political revolution represented by the military dictator and recorded his views in a remarkable study called *Il Principe* (The Prince). The Florentine statesman and historian has often been condemned by people with a gift for indiscriminate indignation under the mistaken impression that he composed his work as a sort of textbook for tyrants. Nothing was farther from his mind. What chiefly moved him was to understand and describe the contemporary Italian situation. But, passing peninsular politics in review, he scorned, as an honest and penetrating observer, to mince matters. In fact with his eye on the Italian states of his day he made it perfectly clear that the successful prince, as distinguished from the unsuccessful one, lived by the inspiration of virtù and that virtù is a special form of manhood requiring its possessor to be alert, energetic, fearless, and absolutely unscrupulous.

And what Machiavelli deduces as the rule of his age for the princes of Italy Cellini presents with unexampled fervor as the proper line of conduct for artists. True, Cellini is less likely to convince us than his Florentine fellow-citizen, because if we know Renaissance art with some degree of thoroughness, we are aware that not all the artists were impassioned individualists. Some of the greatest, like Fra Angelico and Botticelli, never permitted themselves to become estranged from the old religious pieties. As faithful adherents of Christianity and the Church they bridled their restive wills without great difficulty. But in the main the artists, too, sought self-expression as their highest goal; and in some extreme instances, such as that of Cellini, identified self-expression with the wildest personal license. The point of caution about Cellini is that, exhibiting this license at its height, he is no longer fairly representative of his kind. With a vivacity and zest that make his book as fresh today as it was when it was written, he tells us how he forced his way as a metal-worker and a sculptor among the highest lords of the land. The despot had by Cellini's time become the normal political phenomenon not only in Italy but throughout Europe; and it is amazing and amusing to observe how he, the self-made artist, associated with these self-made potentates on a substantially equal footing. His swank and swagger never falter. Far from suppressing his misdemeanors, which include a notable list of thefts, rapes, and murders, he recounts them with an equanimity as if he were enumerating his claims to eternal bliss. Note once again that Cellini is admittedly an extreme instance among artists and that he came upon the scene when the sun of the Renaissance was already declining to its setting; nonetheless his spirit was kindled at the fiery ideal of his age and we may think of him as embodying among artists a genuine, though peculiarly virulent form of virtù.

Permit me in conclusion to offer a sweeping evaluation of the society we have been engaged in describing. Its driving force, we have learned, was individualist energy released by the breaking down of a host of sacred and semisacred medieval conventions. In this way new groups came to the front whose individual members seized upon the opportunities offered by an enlarged world and passionately pursued their personal advantage. The Renaissance is accordingly an age of strong men, of optimates and aristocrats. For hundreds of years down to our own day it has been celebrated as the period when Italy became a veritable hothouse of genius, and on this account a glamor invests it which has frequently obscured its many drawbacks. But these drawbacks exist and may not be overlooked by the social philosopher. They constitute in their sum the inevitable accompaniment of an individualism which, gathering momentum as it proceeded, ended by becoming anti-social and plunging the society which it dominated into anarchy. A disruptive anarchy was the logical consequence of an individualism carried to excess. The too fiercely competitive struggle among giants bent the bow of social order till it snapped to splinters.

A social movement is of course too complicated a process to be reduced to a simple formula. I would not therefore be taken as maintaining that individualism is the single and exclusive explanation of Renaissance society. That society came about through individualism plus a score of other forces and conditions active in Europe at that particular historical moment. And when the energy of the Renaissance failed and the age guttered out like a dying candle, I would not be understood as saying that this extinction was due exclusively to the social anarchy which followed from a too riotous pursuit of selfish ends. However, so much is certain: by, let us say, the year 1500 this anarchy, expressive of an exaggerated and frenzied individualism, is as much the outstanding aspect of Italian society as a more moderate and balanced individualism had been the hall-mark of the earlier and more soundly productive years of the Renaissance.

And anarchy bore its bitter fruit in social dissolution followed in its turn by a sharp reaction back to a normal social order. Whoever contemplates with elation the brilliant array of writers and artists of the period under review owes it to himself, if he is historically minded, to recall that the Renaissance was followed by the Catholic reaction, which made it its business, in the name of a divinely determined scheme of life, to stamp out every spark of free thought and personal daring, until by the close of the sixteenth century the individual wills, once so proud, were broken and the Italians reduced to a herd of bleating sheep ruled by the omnipotent Roman shepherd. The counter-Reformation is, mentally and ethically, a dark and depressing chapter of Italian history. But since this period follows the Renaissance, the conclusion is unescapable that beneath its blinding surface splendor the earlier movement must have nursed the seeds of its own destruction. I am a historian, not a moralist, and I offer no moral conclusion touching this sequence. Abiding by my rôle of analyst concerned with facts and forces, I may however properly conclude my sketch of the society of the Renaissance by pointing out, first, that individualism is certainly the most distinguished agency accounting for the social organization and powerful creative ferment of this period, and, second, that this same individualism, madly overreaching itself, undermined its own towering edifice.

SCIENCE IN THE RENAISSANCE

SCIENCE IN THE RENAISSANCE

GEORGE SARTON

IT IS fortunate that a survey of scientific efforts was included in this series of lectures, for without it our view of the Renaissance would be not simply incomplete—that would not matter so much —but radically false. Indeed from the scientific point of view the Renaissance was *not* a renaissance. That age of tremendous revival, the memory of which makes our hearts beat faster, was a golden age of arts and letters, but to the historian of science, whose curiosity has been whetted by glorious paintings, it is on the whole disappointing. If one excepts the extraordinary climax which occurred toward the end of that period, in 1543, the Renaissance was less a genuine revival than a halfway rest between two revivals. The first of these, which began in the second half of the eleventh century and culminated in the thirteenth, was stimulated by the reception of Greco-Arabic knowledge in Western Europe; the second, which witnessed the development of the experimental method after more than a thousand years of groping, did not really begin before the seventeenth century. The first of these revivals was essentially a re-establishment of connections with the main source of intellectual life, the Greek writings as transmitted and amended by the Arabic-speaking scholars. It is clear that the quickest way to go forward was first of all to assimilate the abundant treasures of knowledge which the Greeks and Muslims had collected. The second revival was really a new start, and to show how momentous, it will suffice to remark that this time, if any, can be spoken of as the beginning of modern science.

The traditional Renaissance, cisalpine or trans-alpine, was a sort of anticlimax between these two peaks. I was interested to find that my conception of it was already foreshadowed by one of most penetrating students of the period, John Addington Symonds, in spite of the fact that he was primarily a man of letters. In the fifth volume of his *Renaissance in Italy*—a work which has almost reached the dignity of a classic (which means that people are more prone to praise than to read it)— he remarked, "The Renaissance in general may be called the Middle Ages in dissolution."[1] He repeatedly insisted upon this. However true this might be from his point of view, it is far more so from our own. And how did this happen? The twelfth century Renaissance was far more con-

[1] V, 392.

cerned with ideas than with words; it was so anx-
ious to obtain and to transmit the substance of
Greco-Arabic thought that it neglected the form.
A perfect translation is an unattainable ideal;
translators have generally to choose between two
evils, a sacrifice of their own language in order to
reproduce the other more faithfully or a sacrifice
of accuracy for the sake of elegance. The medieval
translators did not hesitate, strict literalness was
their aim, and in consequence their Latin was
atrocious. This went on for centuries, and I may
add that the Jewish translators behaved in the
same way, but happily for them it was easier to
translate into Hebrew than into Latin, and less
necessary to twist and torture their own language
in order to reproduce the Arabic idioms. By the
time that the main bulk of Greek and Arabic science had become available to Latin readers, a reaction had set in. These readers had rediscovered
the Latin belles lettres and become more and more
horrified at their own barbarous productions. The
reaction was essentially a literary one; it was antiscientific. In the eternal conflict between matter
and form, the pendulum had swung back to the
latter, and for a century or two, style overruled
knowledge, truth, even morality.

To the leaders of that movement the recovery
of the Latin classics, and later of the Greek ones,

became so-to-say the main justification of life. Everything was subordinated to that great purpose. This is so true that in spite of the fact that three literary giants—Dante, Petrarca, and Boccaccio—had dignified the Italian vernacular and raised it to the same rank as the noblest languages, yet most Italian humanists affected to despise it. Italian was good enough for uneducated people and for women; Latin only was worthy of scholars. This was extremely unfortunate, for however well the humanists knew their Latin, they never knew it as one can only know his own native language, the language that has become a part of his substance even as his mother's milk. However natural it became to them, it remained always artificial to a degree, and so the artificiality and flimsiness of their intellectual life were hopelessly accentuated.

A number of academies were established in Italy, not scientific academies such as those which would proclaim to the world the true scientific renaissance of the seventeenth century, but purely literary ones. The purpose of the academicians was not to discover the truth, nor to discuss weighty problems with a view to their solution, but simply to exhibit the nimbleness of their minds and of their tongues, the elegance of their Latin, and "to make a display of ingenuity by clothing trifles in sonorous language." From the philosophic as well as from the scientific standpoint, this was undoubtedly a regression. As compared with medieval scholasticism, dull but honest, the characteristic philosophy of that age, the Florentine neo-Platonism, was a superficial mixture of ideas too vague to be of real value. The immense efforts which had been made in succession by Muslim, Jewish, and Christian doctors to purify Aristotelian and Platonic doctrines were hardly considered by these supercilious dilettanti; much of the critical work which had been done by their medieval forerunners, whom they could not understand and despised accordingly, was carelessly undone by them. There is one of these Florentine philosophers, of whom perhaps more could have been expected, Giovanni Pico della Mirandola, but unhappily he died before having reached his full maturity.

The antiscientific tendencies of the humanists did not by any means prevent them from being pedantic. It is true the Renaissance was a liberation from many restraints, but alas! not from pedantry. These fastidious literati were perhaps as pedantic as the medieval philosophers, but the incidence of their pedantism was moved from matter to form. They paid far less attention to the definition of concepts and to logical rigor but fussed tremendously about grammar, rhetoric, and diction. I do not say that they were entirely wrong; theirs was a necessary reaction, an indispensable stage in the development of modern science. Galileo would not have thought so deeply but for the philosophical exertions of his medieval ancestors, nor expressed his views with so much strength and beauty but for the literary experiments of the Italian humanists.

With the exception of Leonardo da Vinci the best representative of the scientific spirit in the Italian Renaissance was not a man of science, but, strangely enough, a historian and politician, the Florentine Niccolò Machiavelli. Almost alone in the midst of a generation of sophists, Machiavelli was not afraid of following his thoughts to the bitter end nor of explaining them in straight and forceful language. Indeed his language had already a true scientific ring, and was in that respect an anticipation of Galileo's. The realism and directness of his *Principe* (1513) were truly refreshing. Unfortunately Machiavelli was too much a child of his time to emancipate himself from the vanity and corruption of his environment, and consider things *sub specie aeternitatis*. Hence he could not be a real and complete scientist.

To illustrate the lack of scientific interest of the humanists, it will suffice to recall their cold reception of the two greatest events of the age: the development of printing and the geographical discoveries.

There is no doubt that the earlier humanists, far from being pleased by the discovery of printing, were hostile to it. Their attitude was not unsimilar to that of many humanists of our own time with regard to the moving pictures or the phonograph. A good example of their aversion to printing was given by Vespasiano da Bisticci, one of the noblest minds of the Florentine quattrocento. Although Vespasiano died only in 1498—and by that time the new art was already highly developed —he remained suspicious of it until the end. He himself tells us that one of his patrons, the duke of Urbino, would have been ashamed to have possessed a single printed book! It is true that attitude became impossible in the following century, the more so because the humanists found that the printing press, far from being their enemy, was their best friend and their most generous provider.

As to the geographical discoveries, the humanists not only failed to appreciate their supreme importance, they generally ignored them altogether. New worlds were being discovered, the western barriers removed, the earth, finally encircled— were these not subjects fit to be sung by poets? Nevertheless the literature devoted to these immense exploits is utterly insignificant, and for a real masterpiece, the only one ever inspired by them, we have to wait until 1569 when Camoens' epic, *Os Lusíadas*, was completed. But by that time the true Renaissance and the golden age of geographical exploration were already over.

Happily when great events happen, it does not matter so much whether they are appreciated or not. Their pregnancy lies in themselves and not at all in the imaginations of other people. When the intellectual élite paid no attention to the heroic adventures of the early navigators, it hurt nobody but itself, and proved nothing except its own unfitness for leadership. Such an élite was doomed to change or die, and indeed subsequent centuries witnessed its futile efforts to preserve a supremacy of which it became less and less worthy. The struggle is not over yet, but humanists of the old type are now reduced to criticism of the present in the light of the past; they can no longer lead mankind in any real sense.

Did the Italian Renaissance then contribute nothing to the advancement of science? Oh, yes, it did, but the main contributions, outside of mathematics, were made, not by the élite, but by people of a humbler condition, the craftsmen. These were generally people of little education, for their manual training began very early in life. This was at once a handicap and a tremendous advantage. The boys who had grown up in the workshops of their elders were left in ignorance of many good things and we can readily imagine that their manners were not very refined, but on the other hand they were spared the burden of much knowledge which was useless if not worse. While their hands became more deft, their minds remained clear and fresh. They did not waste their time trying to explain impossible riddles or to encompass the universe with elegant phrases; they were bent on solving the simple problems of their craft. The philosophical riddles could not be explained, but the technical problems could often be solved. And not only that, but each problem led to others, which could (or might) be solved each in its turn.

Our knowledge of chemistry and physics was largely developed in that very manner. The best illustrations may be found in the history of mechanics, for in that field we can contrast the sterility of premature abstraction and the fertility of the experimental method, but this would be a little too difficult to explain in this place, and I prefer to choose examples in two other fields less remote from the reader's experience, perspective and anatomy. The Florentine painters were possessed with the idea of representing people and objects as faithfully and beautifully as possible. The representation of objects, especially of geometrical ones—such as buildings, furniture, and tiled floors, —involved the solution of a number of problems which belong to the art of perspective. The early history of that art may be summarized by the following names, which are familiar enough to all students of the Renaissance: Filippo Brunelleschi, Leon Battista Alberti, Paolo Uccello, Piero della Francesca, Leonardo da Vinci. Note that all these men were artists; their main interest was to solve the limited problems suggested by their own work. These problems were not vague and fanciful but clear and determined by life itself, and therefore there was good hope of solving them. The Florentine artists did not solve them completely but they advanced their solution considerably, and by so doing they not only raised their art to a higher level but prepared the creation of a new branch of mathematics.

The history of their anatomical efforts is not less significant. Under the influence of classical models they rediscovered the beauty of the human body and the aesthetic possibilities, almost endless, of nude figures at rest or in motion. Conscientious and highly trained as they were, they soon realized that to succeed in reproducing these wonders, it was indispensable to have some understanding of the structure of the body or at least to know the disposition of the superficial muscles and of the joints. Some of them, like Andrea del Castagno and the brothers Pollaiuolo, carried on these new studies with so much zeal that they overdid it, and produced drawings whereof the anatomical details are too insistent to be agreeable.

The climax of these investigations on the technique of painting, on perspective, and anatomy was reached by the Florentine Leonardo da Vinci, who was not only the greatest artist of his time, but may be considered also the best symbol of its scientific aspirations. No other man, not even Goethe, ever combined the artistic and scientific ideals as intimately as did Leonardo. And, mind you, Leonardo was not a humanist, but a craftsman. The rare excellence of his accomplishments was due primarily to his genius, but it was due also to his innocence. He never knew much Latin, and in Verrocchio's *bottega* his mind was not smothered with pseudo-knowledge and empty phrases but was left free to develop along its own bent. Whenever I think of Leonardo's singular genius, I wonder how much of it would have survived if he had been better educated and obliged to lie in the Procrustean bed of contemporary humanism.

I shall not attempt to relate the scientific discoveries made in this period because a full account would be too long and a brief one, too dry. Some extraordinary work was done by the mathematicians and mechanicians, Niccolò Tartaglia, Girolamo Cardano, and Ludovico Ferrari. There was also, outside of Leonardo, a distinguished anatomist, Jacopo Berengario, two astronomers, Paolo Toscanelli and Domenico Maria da Novara, and a chemist and technician, Vannoccio Biringuccio. These few names summarize the best scientific efforts of the Italian Renaissance.

However, the greatest achievements were made beyond the Alps. Two of these, which strangely enough occurred in the same year, 1543, were of such immense importance that that year is perhaps the best landmark indicating the end of this Renaissance. To be sure it continued in more distant countries, but as far as its original home was concerned by the middle of the sixteenth century it was already dying. That *annus mirabilis* saw the publication of Copernicus' *Revolutiones orbium coelestium*, which put the earth in its right place in the solar system, and of Vesalius' *Fabrica*, which was the dawn of modern anatomy. It does not follow that modern science began in 1543, for most of the work done in the second half of the sixteenth century was still of a medieval or transitional nature, and for a real beginning we have to wait at least until the opening decades of the seventeenth century.

Copernicus and Vesalius illustrate very well the stimulating influence of the Italian Renaissance. Both came from distant countries beyond the Alps, but both completed their development in Italy. It is true they abandoned her later, yet she was their foster-mother. Glory be to her! Such was her strange fate; she was not yet strong enough to give birth to great scientists, yet she alone was able to nurse the growing genius of the northern barbarians.

To measure the real signification of that wonder year, 1543, and realize that while it closed one period it did not yet open a new one, it is well to bear in mind the limitations of these two scientific masterpieces. While the importance of Copernicus' work can hardly be overestimated (it is, all considered, one of the greatest books in the whole history of astronomy) it was still curiously medieval in many respects. As to Vesalius, his adherence to Galenic physiology, his very blindness to some obvious Galenic errors, prove that his emancipation was very far from complete. And what is more astounding, Leonardo, unprejudiced as he was, could not free himself from the same errors. Although he was one of the most acute observers of all times, he still saw anatomical details, e.g., the imaginary holes in the heart's septum, with Galen's eyes, not with his own! This shows once more that the most difficult thing in science, as in other fields, is to shake off accepted views, to observe with one's own eyes, and think with one's own brains, without brooking outside interference. Indeed, there is nothing rarer than intellectual lucidity combined with perfect freedom of thought. Genius itself is limited, and can only see and be truly free for brief intervals. Copernicus, Leonardo, and Vesalius, great as they were, failed to complete their own tasks. They did not open the door wide but left it ajar for modern science to creep in little by little, and it was only by the end of the seventeenth century that enough new ideas had been introduced into the old structure to make it appear like a new one.

One other great synthesis was accomplished by a Swiss, the bombastic Paracelsus, who combined the chemical and the medical knowledge of his day into a new body of doctrine, and was thus the real founder of the iatrochemical school. His teachings were an extraordinary mixture of sound and prophetic views with others which were crude and fantastic. Yet he was truly original and his popularity being increased by his very defects (for to many people obscurity is a virtue), he deeply influenced the progress of medicine.

Aside from the anatomical and chemical investigations, scientific thought was promoted by the publication of a number of herbals, containing drawings of plants, some of which were made from nature. This was but the climax of a very old tradition fostered in the monasteries of western Europe. A great many herbals, some of them beautifully illustrated, were already available when the printed ones appeared, but in this respect as in many others the press rendered considerable services, not only in multiplying the copies at a tremendous rate but also in standardizing them and thus making their systematic improvement possible. The first printed herbal issued from Mayence in 1484; it included descriptions of one hundred and fifty herbs in Latin, and as many woodcuts equally remarkable from the artistic and scientific points of view. This first herbal was very popular, not less than sixteen editions of it being called for before the end of the century; and it was followed by various other works of the same kind in Latin, German, Dutch, and French. Thus were the achievements of the so-called "German fathers of botany" (Otto Brunfels, Leonhard Fuchs, Hieronymus Bock, and others) prepared by a very long evolution. Before the middle of the sixteenth century two botanical gardens were already established in Italy (Pisa and Padua). The novelty was not so much in the gardens themselves, for herb gardens had been a regular feature of the larger monastic establishments for centuries, but in the purpose. The new botanic gardens were annexed to the universities, and their purpose was professional and pedagogical. Their very existence implied a material improvement in medical teaching.

I have mentioned the value of typography to medical education apropos of the printed herbals. It was not restricted to these, for even before the end of the fifteenth century a goodly number of medical books had already been published. The earliest appeared in Venice, 1471, and the earliest collection of illustrated medical treatises, the *Fasciculus medicinae*, appeared in the same locality twenty years later and was frequently reprinted in Latin, Italian, and Spanish.

However, with but few exceptions, the bulk of the medical incunabula were simply reproducing ancient and medieval writings. The exceptions were bloodletting calendars and regimens of no importance, a couple of plague tracts and a series of treatises dealing with a new disease, syphilis. These came nearest to our modern idea of a medical monograph. Ten of them appeared within three years (1496–98) and were produced by physicians of four nationalities, Germans and Italians, one Austrian, and one Spaniard. The treatise composed by the Spanish physician, Caspare Torrella of Valencia, was by far the most valuable. As Torrella was body physician to Pope Alexander VI (Roderigo Borgia), he had a splendid opportunity which he wisely improved. Within two months (September–October, 1497) he was called upon to treat seventeen cases of syphilis within the pope's family and his court. Out of that fine collection, he selected five typical cases, which he described.

There has been considerable discussion as to the origin of syphilis, and it is likely that such discussion will continue indefinitely. This frightful disorder was not clearly distinguished until 1493 or 1495, and it is held by many historians that it was brought from America by Columbus' sailors. It is, of course, impossible to prove this, but one thing is certain, there is no description of it—in spite of its being characterized by very definite symptoms —in any Greek or Arabic writing, nor in any Latin one anterior to 1495 (the name itself is later still; it was first used by the Veronese humanist Girol- amo Fracastoro in 1530). There were a number of excellent clinicians in ancient and medieval times, and if syphilis had already existed then, it is hardly conceivable that not one of them would have suc- ceeded in recognizing its entity. To be sure, it may be argued that the disease already existed in Europe before Columbus, in other words, that the *Spirochaeta pallida* was already flourishing, but that it was less virulent. Such a line of argument receives some support from the fact that other diseases (e.g., scarlet fever) have been known to vary considerably in the course of time, and that at least one disease (influenza) seems to vary somewhat from year to year. It is equally impossible to prove or disprove such an argument, but it matters little, for whether syphilis existed in Europe before Columbus or not, it certainly did not become a "mass disease," a "social disease," before the end of the fifteenth century. Before 1495, whether it existed or not, it did not count. From 1495 on, it did not simply exist, it made itself felt everywhere, added a new terror to a frightened world, exerted a deep action on medicine and hygiene, and even helped to modify men's conduct and outlook.

I have expatiated on this, because it is the most striking example of a live scientific discussion in that period. The origin of syphilis was discussed almost from the time of its explosive irruption. The humanist Niccolò Leoniceno held that it was an ancient disease already mentioned by the Father of Medicine; most authors considered it a novelty, and the astrological explanation of its appearance was the most popular.

The worst disease, however, was not syphilis, nor even the ever recurring plague, but a mental one, the growing belief in and fear of witchcraft.

It is here that the Italian Renaissance found its retribution for its contempt of science. Superstition is the natural fruit of ignorance and of pseudo-knowledge. It was considerably aggravated, even as physical diseases were, by the lack of discipline, the essential immorality and recklessness of the age. Moreover, the persecution of witches naturally increased their imaginary power and the fear of them. Such persecutions had occurred at various times, but after a bull of Pope Innocent VIII had formally enjoined them in 1484, they became more frequent and more systematic, and the evil grew to an astounding extent, reaching its climax a century later.

Now the only remedy for superstition is knowledge, experimental knowledge, but the humanists would not hear of this or rather did not even begin to understand it. Thus some of the ugliest aspects of that Renaissance—outwardly so brilliant and so gay—were caused by its instinctive resistance to any kind of scientific enlightenment.

Science like religion implies austerity. Not so art, and the history of the Italian Renaissance is there to prove it. For mankind reached then a nadir of immorality, yet, from the purely artistic point of view, it was truly a golden age. On the other hand, though the quattrocento and the early cinquecento stimulated scientific research, the main achievements, with the partial exception of Leonardo da Vinci, were due to foreigners.

It is not true to say (as is so often done) that the humanists introduced freedom of thought. They destroyed some medieval prejudices which blocked the way; they broke some old shackles but introduced new ones; they questioned the authority of dogmas but accepted the authority of the ancients; they tore down cumbersome restraints but replaced them by something infinitely worse, spiritual anarchy; they smothered scholasticism but put in its stead literary ideals too vague to be effective. They looked backward not forward. They created beauty, plenty of it, but not truth, and without truth, everything becomes arbitrary and insecure, and whatever freedom there is, is a sham.

The only remedy which could have cured them was a direct appeal to nature—experimental science—but this was hardly understood until the following century. It is for that essential reason that the Renaissance was not a scientific renaissance but a period of dissolution and transition.

But our appreciation of it must not be too severe. It was a necessary stage in our evolution. It was one of the battles which mankind had to fight to reach a higher level. The Italians were the main victims of it; indeed, it is they who paid the ransom and enabled mankind to go forward. It is only in very recent years that we have succeeded in reconciling the best ideals of the humanists and those of the scientists, the love of beauty and the love of truth. Let us forget the darker sides of the Renaissance, which it was my duty to expose, and remember only its glories. Leonardo da Vinci, imperfect as he was, will remain an outstanding model for all ages to come.

The Renaissance was a period of dissolution, it was also a period of preparation. But in a sense this can be said of every age, for such is life itself.

Editorial Note.—Dr. Sarton explained these views informally in one of the lectures of this series, but he had not put them down in writing. He consented to prepare this summary of them, because his refusal would have spoiled our publication plans. However, he did so reluctantly. He would have preferred to leave his views unpublished until after the completion of the second and third volumes of his *Introduction to the History of Science* (from the twelfth to the fifteenth century).

THE ART OF THE RENAISSANCE

THE ART OF THE RENAISSANCE

GEORGE ROWLEY

BEFORE beginning a discussion of any phase of the Renaissance it is absolutely essential that we should define for ourselves what we mean by the term "Renaissance," when it began and ended, and where this "new birth" showed itself. This is all the more important since there are as many answers to these questions as there are fields of interest. What would be true to the eye of the scientist, might be quite different to the historian, while the student of the classical revival might contradict them both. We shall only concern ourselves therefore with the answers that the art historian would give, and those again have differed with each succeeding generation.

Thirty years ago the Renaissance in art was ascribed by some to Frederick II, since his interest in classical antiquity exemplified Vasari's theory that the rebirth meant a revival of the glories of the ancient world, and by others to Giotto, whose emphasis on human emotion seemed to indicate an interest in the individual. Moreover, in the past, the word "Renaissance" was restricted to the cultural revolution in Italy and to Italy's influence on the art and learning of Northern Europe. Today the pitfalls of the modern approach are even more disastrous than the dangers of the limited perspective of preceding generations since the fashion in history approves vast syntheses, especially of the contemporary aspects of a civilization quite irrespective of its racial variations. There has been more than enough of "northern" and "southern" man, of medieval and baroque "points of view," and of "Gothic line" and "modern color tache." Generalization has united the interlace, the Gothic cathedral, and Dürer into a common symbol of labyrinthine confusion and has identified the fantasy of hobgoblins with things spiritual. However, in fairness we should admit that these attempts to find common denominators have produced certain recognitions of essential qualities, not to be perceived in a restricted locality or in a single aspect of the age. Today, following the German lead, the majority of art historians would summarize the Renaissance in the following manner:

In concept, it was an age of humanism characterized by a new spirit of freedom, a new and grandiose sense of the individual, a new realism in visualizing nature, a recognition of the several arts and the development of their capacities, and the emergence of the artist as a creating personality.

THE ART OF THE RENAISSANCE

In time, it began simultaneously in Italy and in the countries north of the Alps about the year 1400. To this statement immediate exception would be taken by those who deny such a wide territorial scope to the Renaissance. Although these critics might accept Jan van Eyck in Flanders as a parallel to Masaccio in Italy, they might refuse to find the new realism in Claus Sluter, the Burgundian, when his work was compared with that of Donatello, the Florentine, and while admitting that Brunelleschi was the founder of Renaissance architecture, would insist that the contemporary Flamboyant architecture of the north was entirely Gothic. The movement lasted until 1600 and may be divided conveniently into two phases of a century each, the fifteenth century when the north and south developed independently, and the sixteenth century when Italy created the "Grand Style" of the "Golden Age" and the northern countries became Italianized. This grouping together of the north and south from 1400 to 1600, whether warranted or not, will prove fruitful since it focuses our attention upon four outstanding issues in the Renaissance:

I. GOTHIC AND RENAISSANCE: What qualities have Masaccio and Jan van Eyck in common when they are contrasted with the Gothic artists preceding them?

I. GOTHIC AND RENAISSANCE

Giotto desired above all things to add human emotion to the spiritual drama. To do this he created his massive figures, modeled them heavily in light and dark, drew the draperies taut here and there to give a sense of the solid bulk beneath, and animated them with vividly dramatic gestures, all in an effort to suggest a reality which would convey the new emotion. Ambrogio Lorenzetti in the frescoes of the Sala Pace painted a panorama of fourteenth-century Siena in which no minute detail has escaped him so that we see the styles in buildings, costumes, carts, and donkey panniers. Beside these engaging scenes, Masaccio seems bare and unobserving; yet the gulf between him and his predecessors is great, since his innovations are characteristic of the Renaissance.

The first indication of the new age was the astounding advance in the realization of actuality. Masaccio may not have been interested in things but he had the ability to visualize them in a new way since he was able to see nature in particular. For the first time since Roman days, an artist could render a living human figure. This vital quality was attained by Masaccio largely through his treatment of form. In contrast to the amorphous bulk of Giotto with a shoulder barely indicated here and a knee there, Masaccio's figures are organic forms with living structural relationships between the parts. The mass of the body counts as a visual unit with three dimensional planes of depth in contrast to Giotto's swinging Gothic lines. Although both Masaccio and Donatello continue to use the voluminous Gothic draperies, the relation between body and drapery has been established. Where Giotto's drapery touches the figure beneath it, the two seem to be identical, while in Masaccio the body and drapery are independent. That awareness of body in the Italian Renaissance is illustrated by Leonardo's sketches in which the figures are first rendered as nudes and later clothed with draperies. The new reality of the figure as a whole is revealed by the relationship between the figures. When Giotto deals with groups the figures are crowded together and only attain actuality through a sense of mass, while Masaccio is able to give the impression of individuality and separation. The figures of the disciples in Masaccio's "Tribute Money" are surprisingly three dimensional. This sense of independence is attained by the use of the Renaissance discoveries of modeling light, scientific perspective, and individual consciousness. Instead of the arbitrary light and dark of Gothic painting in which the light and dark seem to be attached to the figure, Masaccio's figures emerge from darkness into illumination as if a spotlight fell on them, which gives a striking effect of individual plasticity. At the same time the impression of actuality is increased by the use of a single source of light. Another observation of nature made by Masaccio is probably related to his use of lighting, namely, the discovery that there are no boundary lines in nature. Consequently the boundaries of his figures are edges, but, like all Renaissance artists, he concentrates too intently upon form to make the additional observation of Velasquez that the edges are indefinite and overlapping. Moreover, the use of the single vanishing point in pictorial perspective establishes the figures more accurately in depth and certainly increases the illusion of actuality. Whether the film of atmosphere which separates the figures is caused by the damage of age and damp or is due to Masaccio's experiments in atmospheric perspective, is not easy to determine. Finally, Masaccio's figures seem more real than Giotto's because they are more convincingly individual. Of course in Gothic times the demand for sepulchral effigies existed, as well as for a limited number of portraits of donors or of contemporary notables, but the visualization of actual detail was too inadequate for lifelike representation of the individual. Only the striking features were remembered and those were generally executed in profile, since the Gothic painter could not handle the subtle modeling of the face required for the frontal pose. It should be noted that the profile is the clearest linear definition of the face just as gesture is the linear movement of the figure. In Giotto's full faces the expression depends solely upon the droop or lift of the mouth or the direction of the gaze of the eyes, and his people are not only all brothers and sisters but they have no personalities except those which they derive from the dramatic situation. In the Renaissance, portraits became living entities through the new realism which could render the detailed peculiarities of the individual. Masaccio's disciples in the "Tribute Money" are types, but they show their derivation from observation of actual people, and in Leonardo's "Last Supper" the disciples become psychological studies, bearing on their faces their traditional characteristics. Even the old Christian types tended to become portraits in the Renaissance, and portraiture became an independent branch of sculpture and painting. Similar changes occurred in the north. Jan van Eyck's realism led to an examination of the details of actuality, so that he painted portraits that are convincing likenesses. These innovations in realism and individualism certainly indicate a marked change between the dramatic Gothic of the fourteenth century and the Renaissance spirit of the fifteenth. Is the difference merely one of degree in the ability to represent nature or is the new representational capacity linked with a deeper change in the conception of artistic truth?

The meaning of the term "artistic," far from being constant, varies with each age according to the part which art plays in society, this in turn depending upon the fundamental problem of the relationship between matter and man and man and spirit. In the Middle Ages the natural and supernatural were one. It is not easy for us to comprehend an age in which facts are "rationalized divine thoughts." The Middle Ages preferred to interpret the natural in terms of the supernatural just as our age refuses to accept other than a scientific explanation. Such an attitude, formulated in theology, determined the nature of art. Obviously, the representation of nature will be unimportant because the closer the imitation the farther the art departs from its suggestion of the supernatural.

No Gothic artist is interested in nature for its own sake but rather as a means toward a spiritual end. In the Renaissance, the material world for the first time became the sole inspiration for plastic and pictorial invention. For example, Gothic artists attempted portraiture and the nude as incidental parts of their paintings, but only in the Renaissance could Pollaiuolo create a group of nudes as the sole interest of his picture. The artistic content should be carefully distinguished from the subject matter. The Renaissance, except for the introduction of certain classical and poetic themes, continued to paint the Christian subjects but the artistic content was no longer Christian. The artistic content is the emotion which in the creative process fuses completely with the artistic form, irrespective of all values, literary or otherwise, which may happen to be associated with the content. The subject matter is generally dictated by some demand which in itself is indicative of the age, but the content is the sum-total of the emotional reaction to the subject matter which is motivated by the understanding of the age. In the Middle Ages, when salvation was the chief concern of life and when the sensuous was a manifestation of the supersensuous, the artists consciously or unconsciously, whether libertines or pious monks, created art that was harmonious with the spirit of the time. For Giotto, the creation of forms was inseparably bound up with their spiritual significance, while on the other hand for the Renaissance artists the world of the senses became the ultimate. We are so accustomed to comprehending art in the latter way that it is difficult for us to realize that this conception of art began with the Renaissance when the evidence of nature became the foundation for artistic truth.

This Renaissance absorption in man and his affairs created a new rôle for art to play. In the Middle Ages the demand for art came primarily from the church—to build cathedrals, to erect altarpieces, and to illuminate manuscripts. The fine arts were not distinguished from the crafts; hence beauty in art was the beauty of good craftsmanship to the glory of God. The blacksmith was just as important or rather unimportant as the sculptor or painter. In the creation of the cathedral all the crafts were united in a concerted effort in which sculpture had to be architectonic and painting must accommodate itself to the decoration of walls and altars or to the glazing of windows. Art was indeed the handmaid of theology. In the Renaissance, art became the mistress of princes who demanded palaces for themselves which should be more than fortresses, easel pictures to satisfy their taste and their growing passion for connoisseurship, sculpture for their gardens, and finally portraits of themselves to perpetuate their names and faces to posterity. To satisfy these demands, sculpture and painting became independent of architecture. This meant an amazing change, since each art began to be aware of its individual capacities and limitations. The significance of Donatello, the founder of Renaissance sculpture, does not lie in his advances in realism, nor in his interest in the antique, nor in his experiments in depth, scale, and composition in sculptured relief, but lies rather in the fact that he was the first sculptor since antiquity to face the essential plastic problems of sculpture as an independent art—the free standing nude, the figure group, and the equestrian statue. This feeling for the capacities of sculpture is lacking in Donatello's immediate followers because they made the mistake of confining themselves to relief in which they attempted to vie with painting, but the Italian Renaissance culminated in Michelangelo who conceived even his painting in terms of sculpture. By a parallel evolution the northern Renaissance produced the sculpture of the Détente. Naturally, painting became the dominant art because it was best fitted to express the Renaissance interest in man and his environment. The Florentines investigated form, the Umbrians were aware of distance, and the Venetians delighted in color. Titian was the most pictorially minded artist of the Renaissance and, more than anyone, developed the capacities of painting as an independent art. For this reason he was the beginning of a long tradition through Rubens into modern times. In addition to his contributions to color, he experimented with asymmetrical compositions balancing voids with solids, and in the Pesaro Madonna he foreshadowed the Baroque treatment of the relationship between figures and setting. Instead of the usual Renaissance convention of a smaller architectural scale for foreground buildings in order to preserve the importance of the figures, Titian kept the same scale for both figures and architecture by showing only the lower part of the building. It is not extravagant to say that the Renaissance solved more of the pictorial problems of form in setting than any other period ever achieved.

II. THE NORTHERN RENAISSANCE

What the north would have been without any influence from Italy is revealed by such artists as Jan van Eyck, Roger van der Weyden, Memling, Matthias Grünewald, Bosch, Breughel the Elder, and the sculptors of the French Détente. They represent a greater variety of styles than a similar group of the outstanding Quattrocentists and yet

PLATE I

TITIAN: THE PESARO MADONNA

they share with the Italians in the three essential Renaissance qualities already discussed—a new interest in the world of fact, a new acceptance of that world as having independent value for artistic creation irrespective of any supersensuous presuppositions, and the separation of the several arts.

However, these qualities will exhibit themselves in the north and south in quite different guise because of the fundamental differences between the Gothic and the Classic traditions. Italy's climate, customs, and racial tendencies would never permit her to assimilate the Gothic tradition, and the northern countries could never forget it. In the north the Gothic feeling survived so strongly that the new Renaissance spirit existed only here and there in part and the Gothic modes of expression were so much the artistic language of the north that even where the new spirit appeared it had to tell its tale in the traditional Gothic phrases. For example, the figures of Adam and Eve in the Ghent altarpiece still preserve much of Gothic ideality in their poses and yet Van Eyck's absorption in the world of fact is undeniable; these nudes are works of art in their own objective right. Gothic also is the continued use of multiple vanishing points in perspective, the absence of bodily form under voluminous draperies which are composed in patterns of swinging lines, and the contrast between the naturalism of the head and the idealism of the draperies. In Roger van der Weyden even the artistic purpose was medieval and his Renaissance character was betrayed only through the choice of the individual as a means of expression. Such a combination of medieval spirit and the artistic means of the Renaissance characterized many northern artists, while in the south Fra Angelico was the only example. "Art demands much quietness," said Fra Angelico, "and to paint the things of Christ, you must abide in Christ." He was still medieval in his wedding of the artistically significant with the spiritually significant; he was of the Renaissance in his choice of Masaccio's forms as his means of expression, forms which tend to detract in so far as they are materially significant. Spiritual values in the arts of representation can only be conveyed by symbol or suggestion; hence the lack of close imitation of actuality in the Middle Ages and the rise of realism in the Renaissance.

In general the realism of the north was more discursive and more minute than that of the south. The tradition of Gothic naturalism, so profusely illustrated in manuscripts, illuminations, and the ornament of the cathedrals, survived in the Renaissance in the northern fondness for environment and for detail in contrast to Italy's absorption in the human figure. This proclivity, continuing into

PLATE II

Jan van Eyck: Arnolfini and His Wife

the sixteenth century, bore fruit in the pure landscape and pure genre of the northern countries.
Wherever this discursive naturalism showed itself
in Italy, some historical connection with the north
should be suspected. Medieval Siena was more
akin to the north than any of the Italian centers,
and her interest in setting and in the paraphernalia
of everyday life probably can be attributed to the
influence of the French court upon Simone Martini
and the Lorenzetti brothers. Through geographical proximity, this same quality of discursiveness
was present in Carpaccio and in many of the North
Italian artists. Jan van Eyck's painting of Arnolfini and his wife is packed with incidentals, the
dog, slippers, pillows, fruit, fly whisk, chandelier,
and the mirror which repeats them all again. The
little Dutch masterpieces are indeed the lineal
descendants of Van Eyck with his exquisite rendering of trifles.

The preceding leads us to the second quality
peculiar to northern realism, which is minuteness.
Just as Masaccio's new interest in actuality expressed itself in his study of organic form, Van
Eyck's realism showed itself in a microscopic examination of objects. Each hair and each pore of
the skin was scrutinized so carefully that the visual
unity of the whole was lost in the focus upon small
detail. Even the new element of light, which seems

diffused through the room, is regarded as illumination for each separate object. Jan van Eyck gives us a realism that is more than real. This microscopic approach to objects produces an analysis of exteriors, so that what we know of the character of a Van Eyck portrait is what the painter's eye saw and not what his mind knew. This study of surfaces also results in an interest in texture and color, that is, in the qualities of things.

The most surprising characteristic of northern realism is the absence of movement. After the dramatic gesticulation and richly interwoven figure compositions of Giotto and the Internationalists which Roger van der Weyden followed, the figures of Van Eyck, of Memling, and of the Détente sculptors seem to be absolutely frozen. They are both static and isolated, while the compositional effects are limited and impoverished. The simplest explanation is that the symbolic Gothic figures could be arranged like so many puppets into compositions of violent movement but, when the factual world became the criterion, movement to be convincing demanded a knowledge of bodily organism, and the north lacked that knowledge because of the minute character of its realism. The immobility of the figures might also be attributed to the architectonic tradition of Gothic art. Dvorak advances an elaborate theory that, just as

PLATE III

ROGER VAN DER WEYDEN: LAST JUDGMENT (DETAIL)

in Gothic art the "immaterial moments" united the almost immovable figures, similarly in Van Eyck there is a participation in an intellectual communion. The figures have an "inwardness and collectedness" which withdraw them from daily life because the very contemplation of objects if sufficiently prolonged and concentrated will awaken in us the "apprehension of Being standing above individual will and action." Perhaps much of the "sanctified mood" of Van Eyck's paintings is created by the fact that his people never look at anything, which gives them a curiously removed quality. Whatever the explanation, it is undeniable that in Van Eyck, the most objective of the northern realists, there flowed a strong undercurrent of Gothic spirit.

III. THE ITALIAN RENAISSANCE

Italy made two contributions to the art of the Renaissance. She investigated the principles of nature and she formulated the principles of art. Perhaps both of these discoveries were related to her classical heritage. As we have already seen, Masaccio's realism focused upon the problems of organic form and the placing of form in depth. In contrast to Van Eyck's absorption with the details of the exterior, Masaccio created highly generalized figures whose suggestion of reality was due to the living relationship of the parts of the body with their proper proportions, and to the settings which have convincing depth because of the introduction for the first time of the single vanishing point. His discoveries of the underlying principles of nature were verified by several painters, each of whom concentrated on one problem. Uccello perfected the foreshortening of the figure, placing his bodies in every possible position; Castagno specialized in the anatomy of muscles; and Pollaiuolo analyzed the laws of movement. Finally Leonardo, having assimilated all that had been known before his time, advanced his observations and speculations to include everything from the growth of a flower to the mechanism of an engine of war. This was the beginning of that confusion between science and art from which expressionism has recently attempted to free us. Just what the relation should be between the two is difficult to say. On the one hand the Chinese have shown us that the finest life rhythm is possible without any accurate knowledge of nature, and on the other hand the Renaissance has revealed the magnificence of nature with all her richness and substance which can only be produced through a knowledge of material facts.

It has been suggested by Max Dvorak that a new world of art with its own principles, irrespective of spiritual values, was created by Giotto and that these artistic values became the basis of Renaissance design. However, just as the realism of Masaccio differed from the naïve naturalism of Giotto, is there not a similar contrast between the Gothic and Renaissance conceptions of artistic values? One was unconscious and the other conscious of its principles of art. Giotto's artistic consciousness was still medieval, and his design was born of tradition and the artist's natural gift. What Giotto owed to tradition is difficult to isolate but it is significant that his feeling for form and composition developed after his trip to Rome, where a stronger classical tradition had survived. At any rate, artistic values similar to Giotto's certainly existed in the best Byzantine and Gothic designs. The important point is that probably the only conscious rules of art which Giotto recognized were the rules of the painter's craft. For him beauty was like truth, a part of being—both transcendentals of the world of the spirit—and the artistic values were not separated from all the other values. The formulation of conscious principles of art first appeared in the writings of Alberti. The break is vividly illustrated by passing from Cennino Cennini, who concerned himself wholly with the processes of painting, to Alberti's dissertations on proportion, symmetry, harmony, perspective, abundance, variety, and composition. Alberti asked what comprises beauty and realized that nature can never attain the absolute beauty of art because her beauty is indiscriminate and fragmentary. He believed art to be a law-bound operation and deplored those who thought that the forms of structures must vary according to every man's particular taste and fancy and not be tied down to any rules of art. What are these rules which determine the beautiful in art? Some of them are derived from philosophy and were known to antiquity, and some of them result from observation of nature, although the sources of these rules are rather confused by Alberti according to the context in which they appear. In one place proportion is derived from philosophy and consists of three kinds, the arithmetical 4, 6, 8, the geometrical 4, 6, 9, and the musical 3, 4, 6; elsewhere proportion is determined by the universal proportions of bodies. Proportions are subject to the principle of harmony, since "architects for instance in the elevation of a room which is twice as long as broad, make use, not of those numbers which compose the triple but of those only which form the duple." The conception of the principle of abundance perfectly illustrates the difference between the south and the north. In the north, the introduction of a variety of objects was merely an aspect of realistic interest, but Alberti made it a matter of conscious delight; he said, "Indeed I am pleased with all manner of abundance that will suit the subject represented, for this detains the eye of the beholder and obliges him to admire the richness of the painter's fancy." Abundance is treated as a corollary of the classical principle of variety. It is only natural that the artists of the quattrocento should esteem the principles derived from their own realistic discoveries more highly than those inspired by antiquity. For example, although Alberti used Vitruvius as a source book and copied the architectural orders from him, he cites antiquity rather as giving sanction to his own original thinking than as a model to be imitated. In the Renaissance period the revival of antiquity began with Brunelleschi and Donatello (who used the past primarily as a source of inspiration), assumed an archaeological character in Mantegna, and finally united with the glorification of man to produce the grand manner of the sixteenth century. Just as the first stumbling-block of the Renaissance was science, the second was "manner." When one pose was considered more beautiful than another regardless of its content, the principles of beauty had become so self-conscious that art faltered, since art is a gift of the free spirit. Raphael was the breaking-point and the sterility of the academies was the

debacle. The issue between the principles of art
and the gift of the spirit has reached ridiculous
proportions when moderns turn to the art of the
savage because of its sensuous appeal or to the
drawings of children because of their freshness as
relief from the academic principles of art.

IV. RENAISSANCE AND BAROQUE

A new conception of unity was the outstanding
characteristic which differentiated the Baroque
from the Renaissance. The focus of the Renaissance was primarily upon the individual part and
not upon the whole; the aim was to give each object similitude, plasticity, and composition, and
only secondarily to tie the separate objects together. If we turn to Alberti again as the chief
spokesman for the Renaissance, we find an illumi-
nating contrast between his treatment of the two
Aristotelian principles of unity and variety.
Everywhere variety is clearly defined and con-
stantly demanded as one of the most desirable
attributes of beauty. Unity in the modern sense is
isolated as a primary principle in his discussion of
sculpture and painting. In his books on architecture there is a more adequate conception called
congruity. "The business and office of congruity
is to put together members differing from each
other in their natures in such a manner that they

may conspire to form a beautiful whole." The approach was typical of the Renaissance, not to conceive the whole as a unit, but to begin with each part with the emphasis upon the process of coordinating the diverse elements. Perhaps the importance of the human being contributed to the same end because we feel in a Renaissance painting that the figures are independent of the setting and are arranged within it. The seventeenth century conceived man and his environment as one, and special treatments of light and space were developed to achieve the new artistic unity.

The manner in which this unity manifested itself varied with the artist and with the locality. Just as the strength of the Gothic tradition made it difficult for the Renaissance spirit to reveal itself in the north and the weakness of the Gothic in Italy permitted her artists full freedom to invent new means of expression, the reverse process occurred at the beginning of the seventeenth century. The Italian Baroque was forced to employ the Renaissance language and consequently it is often not easy to detect the new spirit beneath the bombast of Michelangelesque forms and the profusion of classical ornament, while in the northern countries the artists were more free to develop new devices to create an impression of visual unity. In fact, the generalization might be made that the new unity in Italy remained intellectual in contrast to a new visual unity in the north.

Although Vermeer's realism shows its direct descent from that of Van Eyck, the difference in the attitude toward nature of the two artists is unforgettable. Van Eyck's realism is minute and analytical with such microscopic examination that things are seen independently without a visual coordination of the parts. Although the realism of Vermeer is painstaking, every object is bathed in a unifying light which floats behind chairs and tables and plays equally across wall and brocades and faces, so that actuality is given to the space of the room. Velasquez's approach to unity is somewhat more optical. His eye sees that all forms are indefinite and interplaying areas of colored light; not only are Masaccio's edges lost but no section of the picture has meaning without the whole. The effect is increased by optical focus, which lends greater definition to the center of the picture than to its periphery. Even Rembrandt achieves a sense of unity despite his use of the artificial spotlighting of the Renaissance, because the forms are lost in darkness with only the salient features emerging into the light so that the dark and light are inextricably one and the spotlight treatment suggests an optical focus. Although these artists differ in their approach to the problem of visual unity, they all employ the color tache as their method of putting on pigment in contrast to the Renaissance use of line, silhouette, and forms modeled in chiaroscuro. But what of Titian, Tintoretto, and the later Venetians? Their surfaces are broken up into color tache and their light becomes an artistic means of expression; yet the visualization is still of the Renaissance in its conception. Titian was interested in the texture of objects and in the way light breaks up color, but the texture and the color were always attributes of form, which preserved its independence. Vermeer was the first painter to realize that light was not merely something which fell upon colored form but that it was an integral part of color. His eye and perhaps his mind were aware of color values. The Renaissance thought of color as formal or sensuous. The Florentines used it to accentuate forms; Titian often employed it compositionally as in his "Assumption of the Virgin," where a triangle of red unites heaven and earth; most of the Venetians were keenly alive to the sensuous appeal of color being intoxicated by the qualities of things, especially the green, gold, and rose tints of a woman's skin. For Vermeer the color of an object was not merely an attribute of the object but a quality which visually related and united objects, because the color of an object was not only its hue but its value, which depends upon the light in which the object exists. Consequently the light in a Vermeer interior unifies everything in the room. Such an approach means a new interest in nature as a whole and a more scientific visualization which has no parallel in the Renaissance.

Space, instead of being measured in Renaissance fashion, became a reality in which everything has relatedness. Compare Velasquez with Raphael, who was the greatest Renaissance master of interior space. Raphael's spatial effects were achieved either by geometric perspective, by the measuring of figure groups in comparative scale, or by the descriptive treatment of the atmosphere. One feels that the space could be measured in so many cubic feet and that the figures and the space are conceived separately. Velasquez was so aware of the actuality of interior space that he intermingles a foreground figure and a rear wall because they are both part of the same space.

To analyze the difference between Renaissance and Baroque in their conception of outdoor space is much more difficult because it involves the intricacies of three new problems, no one of which was really solved until the nineteenth century. They are the problem of outdoor sunlight requiring a further range of color values, the problem of color vibration, and the problem of unlimited space. Although the finest studio painter of his

PLATE IV

MASACCIO: THE TRINITY

age, Valesquez failed in the "Surrender at Breda," simply because he was unable to retain his impression of the out-of-doors. Piero della Francesca made the best Renaissance attempt at sunlight effects, being the only painter who observed secondary reflections and their alteration of color, but he knew nothing of color values. The attempt to paint "up sun" by Bernini and Claude Lorraine showed the growing interest in outdoor light in the seventeenth century, and Vermeer's "View of Delft" was unique in its approximation to correct values two centuries before the discoveries by the Impressionists.

To the rendering of unlimited space, the Baroque made several contributions. The problem began in Italy with illusionistic wall paintings in which a sequence can be traced from Masaccio to Tiepolo. In Donatello's reliefs and Masaccio's painting of "The Trinity" the floors cannot be seen because the perspective of the paintings was adjusted to the spectator's eye. Mantegna identified the space of the picture with the space in which the spectator stands, painting a soldier who apparently leans over a railing into the room, and an opening in the ceiling through which heads are peering. Correggio's ceiling figures are detached from the architecture and seem to float in the sky. In the Baroque period, Pozzo painted his vaults with superstructures which so clearly continued the lines of the structural architecture and the actual sculpture that it is difficult to say which is painting and which similacrum; and incidentally this marks a new kind of wedding of the arts which might be called the Baroque type. When compared to the achievements of Correggio, whose architecture and figures stop the eye, the effect of space in the Baroque ceilings seems vastly increased by their added illusionism. Nevertheless, the Baroque still painted in the language of the Renaissance, that is in plastic form and commensurate space. The space was measured just as in Correggio by the commensurate distances between the figures and by the multiplicity of the figures which fill the space. Tiepolo in the eighteenth century was the only Italian who really grappled with the problem of unlimited space, conceived visually. The figures cease to be important; they are few in number and are lost in the vast expanse of the sky. They are as flat as the sky itself so that the eye leaps laterally from one figure to another beyond the scope of the opening of the ceiling, and the effect is as breathtaking as a sudden glimpse of an air squadron overhead.

The problem of unlimited space becomes acute in the painting of landscape. Since most Renaissance landscapes were not landscapes but settings

PLATE V

Brueghel the Elder: Autumn (Detail)

for figures, the artists were more interested in the earth than in space. The Chinese name for landscape is "mountain and water painting." Western landscape might more appropriately be termed "land, tree, and sky painting" in view of our dominant interests. It is significant that most Renaissance painters were chiefly concerned with the more formal aspects of landscape, with rocks, trees, and buildings. The effects are rather those of distance than of space and are obtained by the use of geometric and atmospheric perspective. The Elder Breughel and Perugino are the respective exponents of north and south. One searches in vain in the Renaissance for the expanses of Guardi and Van Goyen or the vast sweep of sky one finds in Seghers. Even these men failed to give the impression of space encompassing the spectator. In Tiepolo space is above, in Seghers it is in front, and only in Cezanne does it seem to be all around, which is the ultimate test of the unlimited space.

Humanism was the keynote of the Renaissance. Is it not true that each age attempts to explain itself in terms of its most developed mode of thought: the Greek in terms of geometry, the medieval in theology, and the modern in the physical sciences? The Renaissance interpreted everything in terms of man and his affairs—not idealized man, not man symbolic of spiritual types—but the individual on this earth and of this earth. For art this necessarily resulted in a period of representation since art is a transformation of nature according to the motivating ideas of the age. Therein lay the dangers and the triumphs of the Renaissance. The artistic content varied according to the individual artist's attitude toward the essential problem of representation, whether he was satisfied merely to solve the physical difficulties implied in the new realism or whether he attempted to utilize those discoveries for some further imaginative purpose. Van Eyck and Quentin Matsys in the north and the experimenters, Uccello, Castagno, and Pollaiuolo, in the south represent the normal reaction to the Renaissance problems, and Leonardo and Titian are supreme because they brought the development of the artistic means of the Renaissance to its perfection and also attempted to reveal the subtleties of man's mind, which had been brought to consciousness by the emergence of the individual. The artists who demand most of us are those in which the artistic content is such that it can only be suggested. As we have already seen, Fra Angelico and Roger van der Weyden gave new intensity to the Christian themes by their portrayal of actual people, capable of experiencing the passion of Christ. In Fra Angelico's "Crucifixion," Dominic, Francis, and the other saints are present in the flesh while the artist's treatment of the setting helps to suggest the mystical character of the experience. Matthias Grünewald used his knowledge of material fact to make the agony of the cross indelible. The flesh is horribly lacerated and the very trees are tortured. This awareness of spiritual values diminished as the Renaissance progressed since humanism required that Christian feeling should give place to the poetic fancy of Botticelli or to the color effects of Giorgione which waft us away into dreams of idyllic nature. Finally humanism found its most vital expression in two artists who epitomize the full fruition of the Renaissance and perfectly represent the two extremes of the north and the south in the sixteenth century. They are Michelangelo and Breughel the Elder. Through Italy's passion for human form, man ultimately became a Titan in the hands of Michelangelo, while Breughel, the son of a peasant, viewed humanity with the simplicity and directness of the peasant. Both artists were keenly alive to the tragedy of life conceived only in humanistic terms; in Michelangelo this awareness expressed itself through symbols of man's struggle with destiny and in Breughel through the portrayal of the vicissitudes of every day. The Italian expressed his emotion almost wholly by means of the human nude and the Flem-

ish master, despite his interest in the figures, laid
the foundation for modern landscape. The theme
of the Renaissance was man—in the south his
glorification, and in the north his acceptance as a
human being with all the joys and sorrows, failures,
and successes of this life.

INDEX

INDEX

INDEX

INDEX